What Next?

YOUR FIVE-YEAR PLAN FOR LIFE AFTER COLLEGE

ELANA LYN GROSS

Adams Media

New York London Toronto Sydney New Delhi

To my family, friends, and coffee for always being there for me.

Adams Media
An Imprint of Simon & Schuster, Inc.
57 Littlefield Street
Avon, Massachusetts 02322

First Adams Media trade paperback edition April 2020

ADAMS MEDIA and colophon are trademarks of Simon & Schuster.

For information about special discounts for bulk purchases, please contact Simon & Schuster Special Sales at 1-866-506-1949 or business@simonandschuster.com.

The Simon & Schuster Speakers Bureau can bring authors to your live event. For more information or to book an event contact the Simon & Schuster Speakers Bureau at 1-866-248-3049 or visit our website at www.simonspeakers.com.

Interior design by Julia Jacintho
Interior image © Simon & Schuster, Inc.
Hand lettering by Priscilla Yuen

Manufactured in the United States of America

2 2021

Library of Congress Cataloging-in-Publication Data
Names: Gross, Elana Lyn, author.
Title: What next? / Elana Lyn Gross.
Description: Avon, Massachusetts: Adams Media, 2020. | Includes index.
Identifiers: LCCN 2019059303 | ISBN 9781507213452 (pb) | ISBN 9781507213469 (ebook)
Subjects: LCSH: Young adults--Life skills guides. | College graduates--Employment. | Career development, | Success.
Classification: LCC HQ799.5 .G576 2020 | DDC 646.70084/2--dc23
LC record available at https://lccn.loc.gov/2019059303

ISBN 978-1-5072-1345-2
ISBN 978-1-5072-1346-9 (ebook)

Contents

PART 3 - WELLNESS 145

PART 4 - RELATIONSHIPS 191

CONCLUSION 229

RESOURCES 231

ACKNOWLEDGMENTS 234

INDEX 236

Introduction

Congratulations! You graduated from college! You worked hard, passed dozens of midterms and finals, wrote countless papers, and finished thousands of assignments. You met great friends, sharpened your skills at extracurriculars and summer jobs and had fun.

You learned a lot in college, but there are thousands of things that didn't appear on your Statistics and Probability syllabus that you need to know in life. While you're in school, you have many resources around you: professors, health center doctors, advisors, a career counselor, and all your friends. Once you graduate and leave the comfort of campus, you suddenly have to figure everything out on your own—how to get a job, set up a 401(k), stay fit, navigate your personal relationships, and so much more. It's normal to feel overwhelmed or behind the curve. You might find yourself struggling with these tasks and wondering "Why didn't they teach me this in college?!"

Think of this book as your textbook for life after college. It's broken down into four sections that highlight the key areas of your life: career, finances, wellness, and relationships. In the first chapter, you'll learn how to create a customized five-year plan that defines your goals in each area, helps you stay motivated, tracks your progress, and gives you ample opportunities to celebrate your accomplishments.

The rest of the book is filled with the actionable advice you need to reach those goals, such as guidance on how to land a job, manage your money, stay healthy, and find your "people." There aren't any pop quizzes, but there are activities for personalizing the tips so they work best for you.

I know how overwhelming it is to navigate the first five years of post-grad life because I had my own moments of feeling lost and confused. I wasn't sure what I wanted to do for my career, so I started interviewing people to find out about their career paths and writing about the professional and personal development topics my friends and I talked about as we navigated post-grad life. It turns out that I wasn't as lost as I thought. I had accidentally stumbled into the career I wanted all along—journalism. Since then, I've written about career, finance, wellness, and relationship advice for dozens of magazines, newspapers, and online publications…and now I've compiled the best tips into the book I wish I had when I graduated from college.

Let this book pick up where school left off and give you the rest of the information you need to feel prepared and confident!

Chapter 1

Make Your Five-Year Plan

You can't achieve your goals if you don't know what they are and why they are important to you. The purpose of a five-year plan is to clarify what you want, why you want it, and how you'll make it happen. Your five-year plan should cover all the aspects of your daily life, including career, finances, wellness, and relationships.

WHAT IS A FIVE-YEAR PLAN?

A five-year plan is a road map for how the next few years of your life could play out. It prompts you to think about what you want and how you'll get it. Your plan is customized to you. It will be different than your best friend's, your roommate's, or the one your parents would create for you. The goal is to reflect on what *you* really want—not what other people want for you. You don't have to worry about having your entire life planned out; you'll focus on making the most of the first five years after college because that is when you are creating the foundation for your adult life.

Your five-year plan isn't set in stone. It can and should change as your life changes. You might fall in love with someone who lives across the country, discover a new and exciting job opportunity, start your own business, decide to go to graduate school, or something else entirely. This five-year plan covers all the components of your life, so even if one aspect—like your job—changes, your other goals might stay the same. It's better to have a plan and change it than to not have one at all.

How do you create an actionable five-year plan for all the important areas of your life? Follow these five simple steps, and, by the end, you'll get your game plan for the next five years.

The first step is to reflect on your past and start thinking about the future. Next, you'll brainstorm what your ideal life will look like in five years. In Step 3 you'll create five SMART goals for each of the main aspects of your daily life, and in Step 4, you'll organize these goals into three categories. The last step is to plan for how you'll reach these goals.

STEP 1: REFLECT

Reflect on where your life is at this moment, what you're happy about, what you want to change, and what your personal values are. This will help you understand what you want, identify your strengths and weaknesses so you know a career path that would be good for you, and set realistic goals.

Even if you had different majors, you've been on a similar path as your friends for the past four years of college: You've lived together in the dorms or nearby apartments, eaten thousands of meals in the dining hall, danced the night away at parties, and studied together in the library. You've all had similar goals: getting good grades in your classes, dating, making new friends, landing summer jobs, and having fun.

Now you are embarking on different career paths, navigating new cities, creating new support systems, and shaping your own post-grad lives. It's easy to feel swayed by what your friends are doing, what your partner's plans are, or what your parents want for you. Self-reflection will help you tune out the noise of other people's expectations so you hone in on what will make you feel happy and fulfilled.

Journaling increases mindfulness and is cathartic. Journaling can decrease anxiety and depression and boost your physical health, so try to make a habit of journaling once a day or even once a week. You don't have to write a play-by-play of every day or week—although that can help you untangle your emotions. Look for journaling prompts that resonate with you like the exercises throughout this book. Use your journal to respond to these prompts if you run out of space or to keep all your journaling in one spot.

These prompts will get you closer to creating your five-year plan. Turn back to them every year to see if your goals have shifted and if you want to reassess any of the sections of your five-year plan. These are good for self-reflection because they cover key areas—career, finances, wellness, and relationships—and encourage you to look inward to find the answers. Answer them with an open mind—remember, there are no wrong answers.

Career
- Where do my talents and interests align?
- What did I enjoy doing when I was younger?
- What has been my biggest professional accomplishment so far?
- What are my professional strengths and weaknesses?
- What types of projects and assignments make me feel energized and excited?

Finances

- What do I value more, experiences or things? Why?
- What financial decisions am I most proud of?
- What shaped my view of money and managing my finances?
- What areas of money management do I need to learn more about?
- What has held me back from reaching my financial goals?

Wellness

- What are my personal values?
- When have I felt the proudest of myself?
- What activities or interests energize me and make me feel excited?
- What are healthy habits that make me feel good?
- What are unhealthy habits I'd like to ditch?

Relationships

- What characteristics make me a good friend?
- What qualities do I value in my friends?
- What characteristics make me a good partner?
- What characteristics do I value in a partner?
- How have my relationships with family changed over the last two to three years?

These questions will get you started, and then you can use the many other self-reflection prompts that you will find throughout the book to continue the practice.

Here are some daily reflection prompts to use:
- What are five things I'm grateful for today?
- What are three things I want to accomplish tomorrow?
- How did I support my friends and family today?
- What made me happy today?
- What am I worried about right now?

Reflecting helps you get in closer touch with your emotions, and journaling will help you work through those emotions so you understand them better. Now that you've put your thoughts down on paper about your past and present, think about your future in Step 2.

STEP 2: BRAINSTORM

The next step is to brainstorm. When you plan ahead, you can move forward with set goals. That's not to say you have to plan *every* moment of your life, but having a general idea of what you want will help you stay focused and motivated.

These prompts will help you picture all the aspects of your ideal life throughout the next five years. This is the time to dream big. Start by writing down anything and everything that you believe will make you happy in the future. Don't limit yourself by thinking your goals are too lofty or unachievable. Working toward difficult goals is why you're creating a five-year plan.

Think about the different aspects of your life: career, finances, wellness, and relationships. Write your answers to these prompts to continue to think about your future.

Career
- What career would I choose if money weren't a factor?
- Would I prefer to work at a startup, a corporate job, or on my own business? Why?
- What would I want my ideal workday to entail?
- What specific career goals do I want to accomplish in the next five years?
- Fast-forward to five years in the future. Where do I hope to be in my career?

Finances

- What are five of my biggest financial goals?
- What do I want to change about my current financial situation?
- What are money habits I can start today?
- What are money habits I can break?
- What financial milestones do I hope to reach in five years?

Wellness

- What are five physical health goals I hope to meet in the next five years?
- What are five mental health goals I hope to accomplish in the next five years?
- What is one big fitness goal I hope to complete in the next five years (such as running a half-marathon or completing a triathlon)?
- What are five personal development goals I hope to achieve in the next five years, like journaling weekly, reading before bed every night, or meditating daily?
- How can I step out of my comfort zone more in the next five years?

Relationships

- What do I hope my friendships are like in the next five years?
- What type of romantic partnership do I hope to have in the next five years?
- What do I hope my relationship with family members is like in the next five years?
- What do I hope my relationship with my coworkers is like in the next five years?
- What do I hope my relationship with myself is like in the next five years?

These prompts will help you clarify what you're looking for so you can identify specific goals.

STEP 3: GET SMART

Now that you've reflected and brainstormed, it's time to choose five goals for each area of your life—career, finances, wellness, and relationships—and make them more concrete so you know exactly what you want to achieve. If one of your goals is to read more, you could make a specific goal to read two books a month. One of the popular goal-setting tools is to use the acronym SMART, which stands for **s**pecific, **m**easurable, **a**chievable, **r**elevant, and time-bound, to assess each goal. The SMART exercise transforms broad or vague goals into ones that are clearly defined and measurable so you can create an action plan for reaching them.

Specific

Make your goals specific to be clear about what you want. Take each of your goals and ask yourself these five questions:

- *Who* is involved in this goal?
- *What* do I want to accomplish?
- *When* do I want to complete it?
- *Where* will I complete this goal?
- *Why* do I want it?

Here's an example: You can transform the general goal "save more money" to something more specific, such as "I will put $200 a month toward paying off my student loans. I will save that much money every month by packing my lunch every day instead of going out to eat."

Measurable

Every goal should be measurable, meaning that you know how to quantify if you've successfully achieved your goal. The goal "I will put $200 a month toward paying off my student loans" is measurable because you can check if you saved $200 a month.

Even if your goal isn't monetary, try to find other ways to measure it. If one of your goals is to "date more," you could quantify it by going on one date a week. If another goal is to "get in shape," you could quantify it by challenging yourself to exercise three days a week.

Achievable

SMART goals are achievable, meaning they make you feel challenged but are still doable. If you set goals that are too lofty, you might be disappointed and you will not be motivated to reach them. That doesn't mean you have to abandon your biggest dreams, though. Set the lofty goals as your long-term goals and create smaller ones leading up to them that are SMART.

Let's say your goal is to run a marathon, but you've never run a mile without stopping. Instead of planning to run a marathon this year, make that your long-term goal, have a half-marathon as a medium-term goal, and have a 10K or 5K as a short-term goal. You'll still get to your big goal, but you've broken it down into steps that feel achievable now.

Relevant

Your goals are probably relevant to you because you created them. Still, it's good to check in to be sure that they're *your* goals, not society's or your parents'. You are more likely to accomplish them if they are meaningful to you. To be sure your goals are relevant to you, ask yourself these questions:

- Why do I want to achieve this goal?
- How will I feel when I achieve it?
- How will accomplishing this goal be beneficial to me?

For example, if your goal is to run a 10K, you might be doing that to get in shape, lose weight, or feel proud of yourself for becoming a runner.

Time-Bound

SMART goals have a time frame. Decide when you want to start working on your goal and when you want to finish it. You'll be more motivated to stay on track if you have a reasonable deadline. Setting a time frame will help you stay accountable because you have a specific date in mind, instead of simply saying you want it to happen "someday" or "in the future." The 10K is a great example because you'll have a date for the race on the calendar.

By focusing on the five elements in SMART goals, you've defined your goals and started to create a plan for achieving them.

STEP 4: ORGANIZE

Now it's time to organize your SMART goals into these categories: short-term (those that can be accomplished in less than a year to two years), medium-term (two to three years), and long-term (three to five years). Your short-term goals should get you closer to your medium-term goals, and your medium-term goals should get you closer to your long-term goals.

Career		
Short-term goals	Medium-term goals	Long-term goals
Finances		
Short-term goals	Medium-term goals	Long-term goals
Wellness		
Short-term goals	Medium-term goals	Long-term goals
Relationships		
Short-term goals	Medium-term goals	Long-term goals

You don't have to limit the number of goals in each section, but try to have about the same number of goals in each category so they fit into the timeline.

STEP 5: PLAN IT OUT

Now go through each goal you made in Step 4 and decide if it should be finished in Year 1, Year 2, Year 3, Year 4, or Year 5. Once you have your organized five-year plan, keep it on a pin board, in your journal, on your desk, or somewhere else you'll see it often so you can stay accountable and celebrate everything you've achieved.

--- **TO DO** ---

WRITE OUT YOUR FIVE-YEAR PLAN

Use the following chart or a page in your journal to list your goals for the most important parts of your post-grad life: your career, finances, wellness, and relationships. Use a pencil so you can make changes as you create and fine-tune your plan.

	Year 1	Year 2	Year 3	Year 4	Year 5
Career					
Finances					
Wellness					
Relationships					

TAKE SMALL STEPS TO ACHIEVE BIG GOALS

If one of your big goals is to get promoted to senior account executive by the end of five years, there isn't just one thing you need to do. Working toward a promotion takes many small actions along the way, such as showing that you are a leader, networking with colleagues, managing staff, and exceeding expectations. If another big goal is to make new friends in a new city, you can take smaller steps like asking current friends if they can make introductions, joining organizations in your community, and going to parties and events you are invited to…even when you'd rather be at home watching Netflix.

The key to reaching the big goals you've set is to plan out the smaller things you need to do to get there and to check in with yourself once a month to hold yourself accountable.

Every month, sit down and review and celebrate what you accomplished in the past month and remind yourself what you will accomplish in the next month. Set aside thirty minutes to an hour for this reflection and planning in your calendar so you won't forget.

Write down notes as you review and plan each month so you can go back and make sure you accomplished what you set out to. This table will help you visualize your progress.

	What I accomplished last month	What I will accomplish next month
Career		
Finances		
Wellness		
Relationships		

Beginning with career, list everything that you accomplished in the past month in the first column, big or small. Did you get a promotion? That's great! Write that down. Did you finish a big project? That's great, too, and should go in the column. Some of your accomplishments will be directly related to the goals you set, but there might be some things to celebrate that you weren't expecting, like the project you totally would have gotten an A+ on if jobs had grades. Continue this process with finances, wellness, and relationships.

Now that you've listed what you have accomplished, it's time to look to the future and build on that success. What do you want to achieve next month? Maybe you want to learn more about your new role after getting that promotion or to complete a new project your boss put you on. Whatever it is, write it down in the second column.

Once you have the chart filled out, store it in your journal with previous versions of this exercise. Every month, go back and look at the previous month's goals and think about whether you achieved them. If you did, what did you do to accomplish them? If not, what held you back?

LOOKING AHEAD

You've come so far since the beginning of the chapter! You've reflected on your past, thought about what you want now, created SMART goals, organized those goals, and came up with an actionable plan. Now you are ready to move on to the rest of the book, where you'll learn strategies for making all of your career, financial, wellness, and relationship goals happen.

Points to Remember

 A five-year plan will help you identify what you want, why you want it, and how you'll make it happen.

 Reflect and brainstorm about what you want to achieve in terms of your career, finances, wellness, and relationships.

 Create SMART goals.

Organize your goals into a timeline to help you stay on track.

Check in with your five-year plan once a month to celebrate your progress and plan for the next month.

Part 1

CAREER

Think of this section as Your Career 101: a beginner's course in finding success and happiness at work. Review the career goals you set for yourself in Chapter 1. Keep them in mind as you read this section. The advice will set you up for success so you feel positive, energized, and confident as you approach your job search and start your career. Confidence is the key to getting ahead at work and in life. When you are confident, you feel better about yourself and, in turn, do better work, take on more challenging projects, and communicate clearly. Whether you're in engineering or event planning, the skills you'll learn will put you on the path to success, however you define it. This part will take you from your initial job search all the way to getting a big promotion.

Growing in your career isn't just about the technical skills for your field, and it isn't just about title changes. You'll need to work on many skills in order to be successful, such as writing a resume and cover letter, building strong work relationships with your boss and coworkers, and asking for a promotion. This section will walk you through all of these important skills.

Chapter 2

Get a Job

Finding a job is probably one of the first big tasks you'll take on after you graduate. Whether you know exactly what job you want or you're not sure yet, you'll need to learn the ins and outs of job hunting. In this chapter, you'll learn how to polish your personal brand, spruce up your resume, write compelling cover letters, use your network to find leads, make a great first impression in job interviews, and evaluate job offers.

CLARIFY YOUR CAREER PATH

Before you update your resume, write a cover letter, or tell people about your job search, you need to first think about what you want to do for a living. If you have some idea of what you want, great. If not, think back to summer jobs and school projects or assignments you've worked on in the past. Think about what made them successful, what you enjoyed and didn't enjoy, and how the end results made you feel.

Define What You Want—and What You Don't

Under *Start*, list the things you wish you had done in your p summer jobs or extracurriculars that would have made things bet For example, if you are a journalist and haven't edited other peop work yet, you might look for a role that will let you hone your edit skills or allow you to focus on a specific topic like career advice or w ness. Under *Stop*, list the things that made those jobs and projects ficult so you know what to avoid. Under *Continue*, list the things you done before that you want to do in the future, such as brainstorm and writing articles and promoting them on social media.

Start	Stop	Continue

By writing out the things that have worked and not worked you in the past, you will have a better understanding of what yo looking for as you put together your job search plan. Now you've compiled this information, you can define your professic identity through a mission statement.

Write Your Mission Statement

Your mission statement is a single sentence that says what y professional goal is and how you can achieve it. Think of it like a t sis for a paper: It gives you a detailed and specific idea of what want in your ideal career. For example, your mission statement mi be something like "My mission is to use my writing and market skills to help companies tell their brand story and attract clie through social media marketing." It tells anyone who reads it w your skills are (writing and marketing), what your goal is (helping entrepreneurs build their brand), and how you measure success (by helping your clients attract new business).

CREATE YOUR ELEVATOR PITCH

Once you have a short mission statement, you can transform it into a tool to talk about yourself in a professional setting—this is sometimes called an elevator pitch. Think of your elevator pitch as the public version of your mission statement—it's what you tell interviewers when they say "Tell me about yourself." The key is to have something engaging and memorable to say that explains your background and experience in a minute or less, roughly the length of an elevator ride.

A good elevator pitch will explain who you are, what you do, and the value you provide. Think of it as an expansion of your mission statement. You'll need to customize your pitch for the occasion and the listener, but having a general idea of what to say will help you with the fundamentals so you don't stumble to articulate yourself.

If you are in certain industries like journalism, marketing, or fashion, it is helpful to have a professional website or blog. Platforms such as *WordPress*, *Squarespace*, and *Wix* make it easy to set one up and customize it for your needs. It shows that you're taking active steps in your job search. And it gives you more space to add things like a portfolio, references, and a blog, which give a prospective employer more information than a simple one-page resume.

To start your elevator pitch, think of an example of a significant success you've had. Now identify your main professional skills and accomplishments, and the value you add. Finally, build two or three sentences highlighting those key points. You could say something like

"I majored in marketing in college and managed social media for the school newspaper. I doubled the social media following on all platforms in a year as well as the traffic from social media to the website. Now I hope to work at a social media marketing agency so I can increase sales, traffic, and social media followers for a variety of clients across industries."

Practice your elevator pitch out loud to make sure it sounds natural. Remove any jargon, clichés, buzzwords, or fancy sentence structures that people don't actually use in day-to-day conversation. Your elevator pitch should be conversational, engaging, and memorable. A stellar elevator pitch will capture your audience's attention and highlight your strengths so you'll impress everyone from your interviewer, to someone you meet at a networking event, to your Bumble date.

WRITE YOUR RESUME

The ultimate goal of a resume is to convince the hiring manager that you have exactly what it takes to thrive in a particular job. Your resume is your first chance to show them that you have what they're looking for. Tailor your resume for each application by highlighting skills and responsibilities depending on what the job posting says.

Resume Writing 101

A hiring manager looks at your resume for about six seconds, so you only need to include the most relevant information for the job. Instead of listing every job you've ever had (and all the specific responsibilities of each), you want the hiring manager to be able to quickly see that you have the experience they want. It is easier for the hiring manager to do that if everything is on one page.

Use active verbs like *managed*, *organized*, and *achieved* throughout your resume because they are powerful and show that you caused the results—say, an increase in sales. Active verbs help you make sure your sentences don't use the passive voice. Instead of saying "20 percent revenue growth was achieved year over year," it is more impressive to say "Created a sales and marketing strategy that increased the year-over-year revenue by 20 percent." The first example just says that it happened; the second shows that *you* made it happen.

If you think you can't get your resume down to one page, ask someone to review your resume with you to see if there are any areas you can trim. You are customizing your resume for each job, so for information that isn't relevant, you can just include the title and one bullet. If need be, nix the least-relevant jobs. Your resume is a highlight reel, not a full play-by-play of your work history.

Every resume should have the same few sections: name, contact information, education, experience, and skills:

- **Name and contact information:** This should always be at the top of the page so people know who you are and how to get in touch.
- **Education:** Your education section should include the name of your college or university, your degree, your major, and your graduation date (or anticipated graduation date).
- **Experience:** This is where you add relevant work or extracurricular experience.
- **Skills:** This section is where you list any specialized skills that are relevant for the job and industry.

Each section of your resume shows what you will bring to the role, but there are different guidelines for how each should be organized.

Education

There isn't a rule for whether you list experience or education first. Many recent graduates put education first. As your graduation year moves farther into the past and your job experience grows, you can shift the education section lower on the page. If you achieved any academic honors such as dean's list, distinctions like summa cum laude or Phi Beta Kappa awards, include them here as well, because they show your academic success. Share your GPA if it's above a 3.0 on a 4.0 scale, but leave it off if it is lower.

If you have space, you can include other information, such as:

- Relevant college classes.
- A description of your thesis.
- Any outside certifications you've completed.
- Study abroad information, such as the university or college where you studied, relevant coursework, and any honors or awards you received.
- Extracurriculars like sorority or fraternity membership or other groups in which you took on leadership positions or made another significant contribution (like fundraising or planning events).

Avoid using industry jargon, because the first person to see your resume is usually someone from human resources, who may not be familiar with the terms. Skip cringeworthy clichés like *passionate*, *visionary*, or *people person*. Don't tell them you are these things—show it in your achievements.

Experience

When you're writing your experience section, list your jobs in reverse chronological order, meaning the newest job goes at the top. Include the company name, your title, the city and state, and the dates you worked there.

Describe Responsibilities and Accomplishments

Each entry in the experience section should have a few bullet points describing your responsibilities and what you accomplished. Your resume shouldn't just be a laundry list of responsibilities. Use the limited real estate you have to show the impact you made. The best way to do that is to use numbers because they are memorable, grab people's attention, and sound more impressive. "Developed a content strategy and monthly editorial calendars for a brand" shows what you did. "Developed a content strategy and monthly editorial calendars for a brand, which increased *Facebook* engagement by 50 percent, *Instagram* engagement by 52 percent, and *Twitter* engagement by 46 percent" shows that you were good at it.

When you are looking for ways to highlight numbers, look for examples of growth, frequency, time or money saved or earned, or the number of people you managed or worked with regularly.

Even if you don't work at a job that is easily measurable in numbers, you can still think of creative ways to use numbers in your resume. You could list the number of events you planned throughout a year and an increase in attendance, the amount of people you managed when you were president of your sorority, the number of articles you wrote and edited each month when you were an editor at the newspaper, and so on. There is always a way to add numbers.

Make Less Relevant Work Relevant

Some of your jobs might not be closely related to the industry you're looking to enter now. The key is to show the important skills you learned, such as time management and professionalism, and any growth, such as being promoted or gaining more responsibility. If you're explaining your role as a camp counselor to someone hiring you to be an accountant, you can note that you were responsible for a cabin of twenty thirteen-year-olds and were promoted to senior camp counselor after your first summer. That shows the hiring manager that you worked hard and are responsible.

Using Extracurriculars As Experience
Don't worry if you don't have a lot of work experience yet. You can include your accomplishments at extracurricular activities. Share one or two groups in which you took on leadership positions or learned skills that are relevant to the job for which you are applying. For example, if you were editor-in-chief of the school newspaper, you could say that you doubled website traffic, managed a team of ten editors, and were responsible for overseeing the final edits for the entire paper.

Skills

Traditionally, your skills go last on your resume since the prime real estate should go to what the hiring manager is most concerned with: your work experience and education. You might find yourself listing software like Photoshop, WordPress, or LexisNexis. Programs or services that almost everyone knows, such as Microsoft Word, Gmail, or Google, can be left off; hiring managers assume you know the essentials. Remember to keep the skills relevant. You may want to include a hobby you're particularly skilled in, but unless it's relevant to that specific job, it's better to leave it off. If you speak any foreign languages, definitely include that because it will make you a more attractive candidate for any job.

The Final Touches

If you work in a creative field and want a resume with a more exciting format, save that version for the interview because some types of online application software can't read the complicated formatting. (You can find unique resume templates on sites like *Canva*, resume.io, and *Resume Genius*.) Use a common, easy-to-read font like Arial or Times New Roman and a simple resume and cover letter format for your online application. Always save your resume as a PDF so the formatting doesn't change if someone doesn't have the same version of Word as you. Save the file as your first name, last name, and "resume" to make it clear who it's from right away.

Make sure to read over your resume from start to finish to catch any typos, grammar mistakes, or formatting errors before you send it off.

WRITE YOUR COVER LETTER

A good cover letter makes your application stand out. An average or poorly written letter that's clearly been sent to forty other companies might get your resume tossed in the recycling bin. Write a new cover letter for each job you apply for, one built with that specific job in mind.

A good cover letter shows that you are interested in the company, not just a paycheck, and that you will be an asset. Your cover letter shouldn't be a recap of your resume—the hiring manager already has that information. The hiring manager is reading your cover letter to find out who you are and how you'll help them. There are four basic parts to a great cover letter: the opening, why you're writing, why you want to work there, and what you can do for them.

The Opening

Just like with a resume, the top of your cover letter should have your name and contact information. You can find a cover letter template online or on Microsoft Word or have the style match the top section of your resume for consistency. Remember, however, that this is still intended to be a letter, so always address it to a specific person, not just "To Whom It May Concern" or "Dear Sir or Madam." Instead, check the company website or *LinkedIn* to find out who the hiring manager is and address the letter to that person.

If you can't find the hiring manager, use the head of the department, the head of human resources, or the department name.

Why You're Writing

Think of this section as the introduction to your cover letter, establishing who you are and what the thesis of the letter will be. Begin by identifying which position you're applying for and offering a short summary about yourself using your mission statement or elevator pitch for inspiration. If you found out about the role from someone or something specific, such as an employee or a career fair on campus, mention it at the beginning of the letter to get the hiring manager's attention.

Why You Want to Work There

Next, share why you want to work in this role and for this company. This is your chance to show that you understand the role, organization, and mission of the company.

Not sure where to start? Look at the job description to see what captured your attention. Browse the company's website to check out how they describe the company goals, culture, and position. Find out what ideas or concepts match your career goals. If you still can't come up with *anything* that explains why you want the job, consider holding off on that application.

What You Can Do for Them

Use a sentence or two to explain why you're the best person for the job. Pick two or three of the most important qualifications in the job description and show how your past experiences taught you those skills. As with your resume, use concrete examples and numbers. For example, you can point out that you doubled your *Facebook*, *Twitter*, and *Instagram* followers in just three months.

Closing and Proofreading

Finish the letter by thanking them for considering you for the position. You don't need to say how they can get in touch because your contact info is at the top of your letter. End with something simple like "Thank you for your consideration. I look forward to hearing from you." You can print it, sign it, and scan it, but you can also just type your name to sign off.

The app Grammarly is helpful for catching grammar, spelling, punctuation, word choice, and style mistakes that spell-check might miss. Don't let a misuse of *their*, *there*, or *they're* keep you from landing the job.

Read over the letter to catch any typos and grammatical errors before sending it.

SEARCH FOR JOBS AND USE YOUR NETWORK

Now that you've figured out the types of roles and companies you want to apply to, developed your personal brand, and edited your resume and cover letter, you're ready to apply to jobs. In this section, you'll learn strategies for staying organized throughout the job search, maximizing your network, and arranging informational interviews.

Get Organized

Before you start applying for jobs, you need to get organized. Make a spreadsheet to keep track of all the important details about your application process and update it each time you apply somewhere new. Here's an example to get you started.

Company Name	Job Title	Application Date	Interview Date	Date Expected to Hear Back	Followed Up	Notes

In the *Notes* section, you could jot down if you were referred by someone, need to send a list of references, or any other next steps.

It's easy to forget some of these details, so you'll be glad you tracked them when you start juggling multiple opportunities.

Next, make a "target list" of the ten or so top companies you'd love to work at if the right role were available. The ideal position at your target companies might not be available right away, so set alerts on *LinkedIn* and jobs boards and check each company's career page regularly to see if there are openings.

Company Name	Connections	Job Openings	Applied	Interviewed

Use Your Network

You know the saying "It's not *what* you know, it's *who* you know"? Well, when you're job searching, it's both. You need to be capable of doing the job, but knowing someone connected to that job goes a long way. Whether it's someone you have known for years—like a family friend—or a friend of a friend you've only met a few times, or an alumnus, having someone who can vouch for you and make sure your resume doesn't get lost in a black hole of online job applications can make a big difference.

You might not think you have a network yet, but you do. You know friends from high school and college, teachers and professors, family friends, and anyone you met at summer jobs. If you wrote down a list, you'd probably have dozens of people. If you don't have a job yet, reach out to these mentors and friends in your industry and ask for advice, tell them what you're interested in, and ask if they know anyone at your target companies. If you don't have mentors or know anyone in the industry yet, expand your network by reaching out to alumni and career services at your college, searching *LinkedIn* to find alumni and connections who work at your target companies, and joining networking groups.

Gather Some Intel

When you're breaking into an industry without any contacts, it's a great idea to find someone on *LinkedIn* who could help you or, better yet, through recommendations from friends, professors, or other people you know in the industry and send an email asking for an informational interview. This type of meeting can help you learn about an industry in general, a specific company, or someone's career path.

If you are connected through someone you know, like your friend, cousin, or the person you sat next to at a recent wedding, ask them if they would introduce you. (When you find someone's

LinkedIn page, click "mutual connections" to see who you know in common. Ask the person you are closest with if they'll make the introduction.) People remember what it was like to be looking for their first job, so you'll find that most are willing to share their advice. Ask if you could meet them for coffee, schedule a phone call, or even send questions by email.

Informational interviews aren't the same as job interviews. You're not looking for a job specifically at this point, but you still want to make a good impression. Do some research on the person you're talking to before the interview. Check out their *LinkedIn* page and other sites, then write questions that weren't covered.

Always follow up to say thank you. If a job opens up at their company, they'll be more likely to recommend that you apply and help you with your application process if you take the time to prepare and present yourself professionally.

NAVIGATE THE ONLINE JOB APPLICATION

Now that you've created the perfect plan for finding a job and started to nurture your network, you're ready to apply for jobs. You may not have learned some of the necessary job search skills in school, like how to avoid getting your resume lost in the black hole of online applications; prepare for a job interview; or evaluate a job offer so you choose a job where you're more likely to learn, advance, and be happy. That's where this section comes in.

When you apply to jobs online, your application often goes through an applicant tracking system, which is software that reviews your materials to see if you meet the qualifications for the job. Robots read your resume and cover letter to determine if your application goes to the next phase of the process, a hiring manager.

This process makes it easier for hiring managers to sort through hundreds of job candidates, and, luckily for you, it will make your application stand out if you know how to get past the robots. You'll have to customize your resume and cover letter for every application, but you'll be more successful if you put in the extra work.

Know the Right Keywords to Include

Applicant tracking systems review your application to see if it contains keywords and phrases in the job description. Read the post to find out the exact terms and qualifications that are necessary for the job—those are likely the keywords that the hiring manager has told the software to look for. Don't copy half the job description word for word, but use some of the important phrases from it in your resume and cover letter. When the system scans your application, it will pick up the similar keywords and phrases and pass it to the hiring manager.

One key point to remember is that robots don't understand nuance as well as humans. Your title at your previous job might have been something creative, but the robot is looking for the standard equivalent. When you send in your application, it's better to simplify your job title so it gets picked up. Your fancy title is a great conversation starter, though, so you can use it for the resume you bring to your interview.

ACE YOUR JOB INTERVIEWS

The hiring manager needs to meet you to determine if you're the right fit for the role.

Remember that you got the interview because the hiring manager thinks you have the skills to do the job. Use that knowledge to boost your confidence. If you're not confident in yourself, the interviewer won't be either.

Before Your Job Interview

You might think you're good at winging it, but for something as important as a job interview, it is definitely better to prepare first. The good news is you'll likely know most of the questions in advance. Prepare for the most common interview questions and write out bullet-point answers so you know the main talking points for each. When the interviewer inevitably asks one of the questions, you'll have a response ready.

Now conduct a practice interview. Ask a friend or family member to be your mock interviewer. Have them ask you some of those interview questions, and practice responding to any natural follow-up questions they may ask based on your answers. A good interview will be a conversation, so you should expect some back-and-forth. Don't show up to an interview with memorized answers. It can seem inauthentic, and you might get stuck if you "forget your line." You'll come across much more professionally if you've thought about your accomplishments and education in advance and are able to talk smoothly through any answer.

Finally, do your research before any interview. Check out the company's About page on its website to learn basic information like when the company was founded, how it defines what it does, and the mission or values of the organization. And take a look at the company's social media channels—it's a quick way to figure out its point of view on business news and see team events.

As you're going through the company's website and social media, try to get a feel for the office dress code and plan what to wear to the interview. It's better to be overdressed than underdressed for a job interview. Take cues from some of the higher-ups on the company's About page who identify as the same gender as you.

If they're wearing a nice suit and conservative tie or a skirt suit and heels, wear the same to the interview. If they're dressed more casually, be a bit more relaxed by wearing a tie with a nice pattern or a colorful blouse.

During Your Job Interview

When you go to your interview, arrive ten to fifteen minutes early. You may have to find a place to park, figure out where the actual office is in a large building, or go through security, and the last thing you want to be is late. Think about it this way: If you're there too early, all that happens is you make some small talk with the receptionist. If you're late, you've missed out on the job.

Don't ask about the paid time off policy or the salary at this early stage. That would be like asking about marriage on a first date. Wait until you land the job or get further along in the hiring process.

Your handshake starts the interview, so make sure that it is a firm, confident handshake. Present yourself as confident—sit up straight, try not to fidget, and keep eye contact. Ask relevant questions to show that you've researched the company and the role. As the interview is wrapping up, ask what the next steps are in the hiring process and when it would be appropriate for you to follow up.

PREPARE FOR TEN COMMON JOB INTERVIEW QUESTIONS

You don't know exactly what is going to happen in your job interview. But you can be prepared to talk about common interview topics, which are likely to come up whether you're interviewing at a corporate job or a startup. Write notes for each question in your journal, then practice answering them aloud.

1. Out of all of the candidates, why should we hire *you*?
This is your chance to pitch yourself. What makes you right for this job? Talk directly about your specific skills and how they translate to the position.

2. What do you consider to be your biggest achievement? How did you accomplish it?
Talk about an achievement that is relevant to the job you're interviewing for so they can see how you'll thrive in your new position.

3. Why do you want to work here?
The interviewer wants to hire employees who are enthusiastic about their work and the company. Research the company's values and use them in your answer.

4. Tell me about a time when you disagreed with a decision your boss made. How did you handle it and what did you do?
The interviewer wants to know how you handle conflict in the workplace. Think of a situation when you handled a disagreement professionally. Finish the story by telling the interviewer how everything worked out in the end.

5. Walk me through a tough decision you've made in the past six months. How did you end up deciding what to do?
Everyone faces difficult decisions, and the interviewer wants to make sure your judgment is good in these situations. Choose a story with a positive ending, where the tough decision was also the correct one.

6. What are your biggest professional strengths?
Make sure these are relevant and specific to the job at hand. If you're interviewing for a position that mostly involves working solo, highlight your skill as a self-starter, not your interpersonal skills.

7. What are your biggest professional weaknesses?
Don't do the clichéd thing and talk about a weakness that's actually a strength. Your biggest weakness isn't that you care too much about your job. Pick an actual weakness, but one that isn't essential to the job and one that you're working to improve. Explain how you're improving; for example, you are taking a class.

8. If you were given infinite resources to move Mount Fuji one mile east in one year, how would you go about it?
Interviewers like to ask unusual questions like this to test your logical thinking and planning skills. Take a few seconds to come up with an effective plan. Be as comprehensive as possible—don't just explain how you would physically move the mountain; take into account what you would do about the plants and animals that live there. Do the same for any other strategy interview questions.

continued on next page

9. What are your salary expectations?

This is a tough question to answer. You don't want to go too low, but you also don't want to ask for too high an initial salary. Research to find out the average salary for similar positions in the industry, then add a bit more to give yourself some negotiating room.

10. Do you have any questions for me?

Don't waste this opportunity by saying you don't have any questions. Prepare a few in advance that are specific to the company, their products, or their mission. Ask what would make someone successful in the role and then explain how you have those skills or experiences. Ask about the hiring timeline and when you can follow up.

After Your Job Interview

Write a thank-you email the same day as your interview. A thank-you note isn't just polite; it also gives you another chance to show that you are interested in the company and why you're a great fit. Try something like this: "Thank you for taking the time to meet with me today. I enjoyed learning more about [the company] and [the role]. [A sentence about why you're excited about the opportunity to work at the company.] I think that my experience with [your skills that would be relevant to the job] means I could contribute to the team right away." (You can follow up with a handwritten note as well, but send an email right away since there is always a delay with mail.)

Your future boss will ask for references if you make it far enough in the process. Tell your references about the company and role in advance and ask if they are comfortable being a reference. It's polite and gives them helpful context so they know what to say to help you get the job.

If you don't hear back right away, don't panic. There are so many factors that go into any decision, let alone one as big as bringing someone new on board. Wait until the time the interviewer said it would be appropriate to follow up, then send an email thanking them again for meeting with you, reiterate that you are still interested in the position, and mention that you want to check in on the timeline for the hiring process. If you have any updates—like that you took a certification course or went to an industry conference—share them too.

EVALUATE A JOB OFFER

Everyone wants to be wanted, and it's easy to get so caught up in the excitement of getting a job offer that you don't stop to think if it's actually the best fit for you. Before you say yes, ask yourself these questions.

Will You Enjoy the Work You'll Be Doing?

You won't enjoy every single aspect of your job, but think about what you'll be doing most of the time and whether it is something you are good at and will enjoy. Self-awareness is key here. Think about your strengths and weaknesses. You're smart and capable and you can be good at anything if you try hard enough, but you'll be more successful and happier if you have a job that plays to your strengths.

What Is the Company Culture Like?

Are people competitive with one another or collaborative? Are they friends outside the office? Is the company mainly hierarchical or flat? Do you think you'll get along with your would-be boss and team based on the people you've met so far?

You might not have the answers to all of your questions, but you should be able to get a feel from your interviews, the time you've spent meeting the team at interviews, and reviews on sites like *Glassdoor* and *Indeed*. Since you're going to be spending so much time at work, you want to make sure you fit into the culture.

How Are the Finances?

Decide whether you can live comfortably on the salary you are offered. Take into account the employee benefits package, which usually includes health insurance, paid time off, and a 401(k) plan. A company might offer to match any 401(k) contributions you make, which will help you increase the amount you save for retirement.

Try to figure out if the company is generating revenue and if it's profitable. If it is a big corporate company, that may not be an issue, but it's something to consider if you sign on with a startup. There is no such thing as total job security, but there is more of it at a company that isn't struggling financially.

CONGRATULATIONS!

The job search can take a while, but it'll be worth it once you land a great job at a company you're excited to join. Continue to keep your resume and *LinkedIn* page up to date—you never know when a new opportunity will come along.

Points to Remember

- Think about what you've liked about previous positions and what you'd want to change, then look for jobs that match.

- Write a mission statement that captures your professional identity.

- Create a resume and a cover letter that is customized for the job to show why you're a good fit—and get past the applicant tracking system.

- Everyone has a network. Use yours to make connections that could lead to a job.

- Prepare for job interviews by practicing common questions.

Chapter 3

Master the Basics of the Working World

You got a job! Now it's time to impress your boss and other coworkers by being your best professional self and mastering the basics of office life. Getting organized, being friendly, and having a strong work ethic will make you successful. These skills will help you throughout your career, not just in this job.

ORGANIZE EVERYTHING

If you have everything in its proper place, you can get that important paperwork over to your boss as soon as she asks for it or find that key email that has all of the details on the project you're working on. Organization doesn't have to be a difficult task—in fact, it shouldn't take you much time at all.

Your Files

Start by looking through the different areas of your physical and digital workspace and find the right place for every important file.

Paper Files

Even in the digital age, it's easy for paperwork to pile up on your desk. But storing it in stacks isn't very efficient. Instead, create folders for each big project and another one for important paperwork, such as employment documents and annual reviews. Keep the folders up to date, adding new files as they come in and recycling outdated files that are taking up space. Once you finish a project, archive the folder in a file cabinet or shelf. This will create more space at your desk but still give you access to the folder if you need it.

If you don't want to keep physical files, scan them and put the electronic files in folders on your computer desktop.

Digital Files

Just like you would with hard copy files, organize your digital documents with folders, one for each project and one for important work documents. The benefits of having everything digitally available is that you can email files to coworkers, access your documents from anywhere, and avoid clutter. Create an organization system that works for you, like having a folder for every project and subfolders that make sense for your tasks. Name your documents something descriptive so you can search for them and find them in seconds instead of searching folder to folder.

If the documents contain sensitive information, you can password-protect them before filing them on your computer or hitting "send." You can back up digital documents onto a cloud or external hard drive.

Your To-Do List

When you have a to-do list that's longer than a CVS receipt, it can be hard to stay organized. It can be a little extra work, but when you're overloaded with things to do, it's helpful to create a few different lists. Keep one long master list to write everything down as soon as you think of it. A paper list is convenient when you have your notepad handy, but a digital one on your phone makes it easy to access from anywhere and check things off on the go.

Once you have your master list, break it down into smaller lists. This is especially helpful if you're overwhelmed. Instead of staring at a seemingly never-ending list, you're looking at a shorter, more manageable, less stress-inducing list. You may want to have one for repeating weekly tasks like a team meeting and one for all the elements of a big project. If there are any tasks that need to be done by a certain date, write the date down next to the task. You can make another weekly to-do list for everything that needs to be done that week.

Now take your lists and organize each one by priority. If something doesn't need to be done by a certain date or isn't as important, keep it at the bottom of your list so you tackle the most important things first. Continue to update the list as things change and new items are added.

Spending a few minutes on Sunday or Monday to make a list will go a long way to getting you organized for the week.

If you're really swamped on a certain day, take a minute in the morning to make a list for just that day. This helps you prioritize your day and figure out exactly what needs to get done.

MAKE A 1-3-5 TO-DO LIST

The 1-3-5 is a type of daily list that works for many people. It makes your to-do list more doable and streamlined, so you focus on what is most important and have the satisfaction of checking everything off your list in a day instead of barely making a dent. Choose one big thing, three medium things, and five small things to complete each day. Write them all down, and try to get the big thing done first.

1 Big Thing

* _____

3 Medium Things

* _____
* _____
* _____

5 Small Things

* _____
* _____
* _____
* _____
* _____

MASTER PRODUCTIVITY AND TIME MANAGEMENT

Two of the most important skills for success at work are productivity and time management. You need to be able to multitask and get things done both quickly and well. You may have to shift seamlessly from preparing for a big marketing meeting to editing a pitch deck all in the same hour. These productivity and time management techniques can make things go smoothly.

Eliminate Distractions

Distractions are a huge time waster. Turn off your phone (or keep it in your bag), dismiss group Slack messages, and resist the temptation to scroll through *Snapchat*, *Instagram*, *Twitter*, or *Facebook*. When you get distracted by something mid-project, it takes time to refocus and get back in the zone. It leads to making more mistakes because you're not sufficiently focused on the task at hand.

If you want to audit exactly how you're spending your time—and where you're procrastinating—download RescueTime. It allows you to temporarily block the sites that distract you most so you are less tempted and more focused.

You can't control every minute of your day, so don't worry if coworkers occasionally come by to chat, you get an email you can't ignore, or your manager pops in with an unexpected assignment. Control what you can and reward yourself with a short break when you finish something or get to a logical stopping point.

Time Management

You need to know when and how to prioritize your tasks based on your deadlines and how important the project is to your boss and team. If you have any questions, it is better to ask for clarification up front than to find out a task was important when someone asks for it...and it was the last thing on your to-do list.

As you work, focus on one task or one type of task—like answering your emails or responding to voicemails—at a time. You can block time in your calendar for each task and receive reminders when it's time to move on to the next one.

Keep all your deadlines in your calendar or a task management app on your phone or computer so you get notifications far enough in advance that nothing gets lost in the shuffle. There will be last-minute projects (the ones that you get at 6 p.m. that have to be done by the next morning), but whenever you have the ability to avoid a quick turnaround, plan ahead. Just like with college papers you started only a few hours before the due date, you're more likely to make mistakes or turn in work that's not your best when you are rushing to get it in. Set pre-deadlines for yourself so you have a day or at least a few hours to proofread everything, double-check it, and make sure it is good to go before handing it in to your team.

FOCUS ON YOUR COMMUNICATION SKILLS

No one works alone, so you'll need to be able to share your ideas effectively. Whether you communicate at work using Slack, email, video conferencing, text messages, phone calls, in-person conversations, or all of the above, the key is to be clear, concise, and professional. You convey confidence—and feel more confident—when you are a strong communicator. Nonverbal cues are often overlooked but affect how you and other people are perceived. The advice in this section will help you to get your point across effectively.

Be Prepared

Sometimes, you'll know that a conversation or important meeting is coming. In those cases, take a few minutes to brainstorm what you want to say. Similar to how you prepared in advance for job interviews, you'll feel more confident if you've thought about what you want to say ahead of time. To avoid sounding too rehearsed or robotic, don't write a script; just jot down a few bullet points so you go into the conversation with a plan. By knowing what you want to say in advance and having a rough plan of the conversation, you'll feel more in control and won't struggle to think of the right response.

Of course, you won't *always* be able to plan in advance because you won't always know the conversation topic in advance, like when a coworker comes by to chat or a client calls with an urgent question. But you can still be prepared by having your desk and files organized and ready to access when you need them. You can grab the necessary project folder or access client files quickly, which will help the conversation be more productive.

Listen Actively

Effective communication isn't just about *saying* the right things. It's also about listening to what others are saying. While it's easy to zone out or answer texts during a meeting or a conference call, try to always be present. If it will help you avoid temptations, instead of bringing your computer to meetings, bring a notebook and write down key takeaways. If there is something you need to do, star it so you remember that it's an action item. Listening attentively encourages you to raise questions in the moment, rather than having to ask after the meeting. This way, you'll have all the info you need.

Write Clear Emails

When your inbox is overflowing, it's tempting to write a few quick emails and send them off without rereading them. Avoid the temptation to hit "send" too soon and take a second to scan for typos, correct grammar and spelling errors, and double-check that you attached the right documents. Not only is it frustrating to realize—too late—that you misspelled someone's name or gave the wrong dates; it makes you look unprofessional.

Set up the "undo send" feature on Outlook and Gmail. It gives you a few seconds to edit or delete your email even after you hit "send," so you avoid that sinking feeling after sending a message too soon.

Use these tips when you're writing emails:

- Use clear and concise language.
- Make your emails as readable as possible by formatting with shorter paragraphs, bullets, or numbered lists.
- Pretend you are the person reading the email to ensure that you've provided enough context and that any action items you need are clearly requested.
- Use a descriptive subject line.
- If you're emailing someone for the first time, introduce yourself in the first sentence or two.
- In that first email, always use an appropriate greeting and sign-off. If you are in a long email thread with coworkers and you notice they drop the greeting and sign-off, you can too.
- Be wary of using exclamation points, emojis, or unnecessary clichés or phrases like "I hope this email finds you well," "Looking forward to your response," or "Thanks in advance."

You'll send thousands of emails during your career, so getting into good habits from the start will ensure that you can collaborate well with your coworkers and be viewed as a strong communicator.

Social Media Dos and Don'ts

There are perks to using social media, but it's a good idea to reassess how you're using it to make sure you're putting your best foot forward, professionally. It takes a lifetime to build a reputation, but it can be diminished in five minutes by an unfortunate post. Luckily, the pitfalls are avoidable. Here's how to use social media responsibly and avoid stressing out because your boss found your not-so-subtle tweet.

- **Do** go through a few years of your social media posts to make sure everything is appropriate. Check posts your friends have tagged you in. A good rule of thumb is that if you wouldn't want your parents or grandparents to see it, don't post it.

- **Don't** complain about your coworkers or your job. We all have bad days at work…but your day will get a lot worse if you blow off steam and imply, or downright say, that you hate your job and your boss finds out.

- **Do** think before you post. Remember that everything is screenshot-able, meaning that someone can screenshot your *Snapchat* or any other social media post, even if you delete it later.

- **Don't** make it all about you and your posts; interact with people and be supportive. Join conversations and groups, share other people's posts, congratulate people, and use social media to promote other people's projects and goals.

- **Do** use hashtags on *Twitter* and *Instagram* if you want to grow your following. You can find relevant hashtags by seeing what other people in your industry use or using a tool like Hashtagify.

- **Don't** accept *Facebook* friend requests from people you don't know. Do you really want a stranger knowing specific details of your life?

- **Do** set privacy settings like controlling how much people can see if they are not connected to you on a particular site. For example, you can change your *Facebook* settings so that you have to approve photos and posts before they are tagged to your page. This way you can prevent someone from posting an embarrassing photo to your page for everyone to see.

- **Don't** rely on privacy settings, though. Even if your profile is set to private, there might still be ways that people can see your content (maybe because they have friends in common or because someone who follows you screenshot your post and shared it without your knowledge).

- **Do** promote yourself. Share accomplishments like getting promoted, landing a big client, speaking at an event, or receiving an award.

- **Don't** post without knowing the full story. If you want to weigh in on trending topics and hashtags, find out why they are trending and the context before you post so you don't get pulled into a conversation you didn't expect. There are doctored videos, conspiracy theories, and other untrustworthy content online. Do your research before you share it.

- **Do** proofread before you post. Quickly check your posts for typos and grammar and spelling errors. Even if you are posting on your personal social media profiles, these posts are still a reflection on you, so try your best to avoid mistakes.

- **Don't** assume that you are anonymous. Sometimes people give in to an impulse and write mean comments on social media posts and articles. If you don't have anything nice to say, whether about work or not, don't say it at all. If someone is writing mean things to you on social media or harassing you in any way, block them and report them immediately.

- **Do** be careful about giving someone clues to your address or the places you visit often, like your favorite coffee shops and restaurants. (If you want to be terrified, but entertained, read the book *You*, a thriller about stalking in the digital age, or watch the television show based on it.)

> Be mindful about what you share on social media about work. Don't share anything that isn't public knowledge, don't reveal that you are looking for a new job, and don't post photos of yourself at the beach *enjoying* the weather when you've called in sick to say that you're *under* the weather.

IMPROVE YOUR PUBLIC SPEAKING SKILLS

Think of public speaking as Communication 102. It's more advanced than email writing, but it's an important skill. When you can get in front of a crowd—or even just one VIP like your boss or client—and speak confidently, it increases everyone's confidence in you (especially because they know how nerve-wracking it is to be the center of attention).

It's normal to feel nervous about public speaking, but just like any other skill, you can get better with practice. It doesn't matter if you're speaking to an auditorium of people, a crowded conference room, or one key stakeholder—when the stakes are high, your body might react accordingly, with sweaty palms and a shaky voice.

Sound Confident

The simplest way to gain confidence is to act and speak confidently. Of course, you might not actually *feel* confident in every situation, especially when you are just starting your career, and that's okay. The good news is that if you act confident, you'll become more confident.

When you're speaking to a group or an important person, use an authoritative voice, speak slowly, and remove filler words and qualifiers. Everyone has filler words or phrases they are prone to use when nervous, such as "You know," "Um," or "Like." They make you feel and sound less mature and confident, but if you prepare the conversation in advance and speak slowly and deliberately, it's easier to avoid these verbal crutches. Skip phrases such as "This might be a bad idea," "I could be wrong," or "If that makes sense," which make it seem like you aren't confident in your idea.

Practice

You don't know what your presentation is going to sound like until you hear it out loud for the first time. Practice your speech or what you want to say in front of a friend or family member. Ask them to give you honest feedback and tell you if there's anything they would change. This will give you a chance to work on the tone and the speed of your presentation. When you're nervous, you're likely to speak quickly without realizing it, subconsciously trying to get it over with. Slow down, pause strategically, and make eye contact with people in the room.

If you're presenting an actual speech, it's fine to bring a notecard or piece of paper with you to glance at. Just knowing it's there will make you feel more in control. If you're going into an important conversation, write down your talking points so if you start to blank on what you want to say, you can reference your notes.

Get in the Zone

Right before your presentation or important conversation, do something that makes you feel confident and less nervous. Listen to your favorite pump-up song or give yourself a quick pep talk to get your mind off your nerves. As you go up for your presentation, inhale slowly through your nose and breathe out through your mouth four times to help you relax. Now that you're prepared and relaxed, you're ready to get up there knowing you are going to give a great presentation.

PERFECT YOUR PROBLEM-SOLVING SKILLS

Another thing all successful people have in common, regardless of industry, is that they are good at problem-solving. The ability to overcome obstacles shows that you are proactive, independent, and able to strategize well, and it's helpful at every level of your career. You can develop your problem-solving skills by observing and analyzing problems, discovering solutions and making decisions, and implementing the solution you've identified.

Observing Problems

Whether you're problem-solving on a big scale (identifying ways to make projects more efficient or generate more revenue) or on a small scale (looking for ways to make your workday more efficient, like prioritizing your assignments if you're feeling overwhelmed), look objectively at the processes, people, and variables that are involved.

Discovering Solutions

It's not enough to simply observe problems; you also have to be able to identify solutions. When you are coming up with solutions, ask yourself why the situations you observed are problematic. If meetings are inefficient, for example, ask why. Is it because people don't come to meetings prepared? Are people annoyed because the meeting topic could be covered in an email instead? List all the possible "whys."

The list of "whys" should naturally lead you to solutions. If people are coming to the meeting unprepared, one solution might be to assign tasks ahead of time. If people are distracted, set up meeting etiquette guidelines like placing phones in a basket.

At this stage, communication is important because if your solution involves other team members, you'll have to be able to clearly explain the problem and your solution. Your coworkers might be able to suggest some "whys" and offer their ideas.

Implementing Solutions

Now that you've observed the problem, discovered solutions, and secured any necessary buy-in, you are ready to figure out how to implement the solution. Make a list of necessary steps in order and the roles of any team members involved.

The ability to identify a problem and come up with solutions is a sign that you have leadership skills. Anyone can complain about a problem, but successful people take the next steps of brainstorming and implementing solutions.

Points to Remember

- Getting organized, avoiding distractions, and appropriate use of social media are essential.

- Creating to-do lists will help you prioritize so you are doing the most important work first.

- You'll need to be able to communicate your ideas effectively. The key is to be clear, concise, and professional.

- Being seen as a problem-solver will help you get ahead at work.

Chapter 4
Decrease Work Stress

Work can be stressful at times. You'll encounter difficult coworkers, late nights, tight deadlines, confusing and challenging projects, and frustrating emails. The good news is that there are plenty of ways to decrease stress, take care of your health, find work-life integration, and take advantage of your job's benefits.

MANAGE COMMON OFFICE STRESSORS

No matter the source of your work stress, the key is to figure out how to mitigate it. Here are some common scenarios and potential solutions to lessen your stress:

- If you are overwhelmed by unrealistic deadlines and a to-do list that is a mile long, you can meet with your boss to discuss your workload; see how long your assignments should take and figure out if there are ways to prioritize, delegate some of your work, or shift deadlines.

- If a coworker constantly takes credit for your work, you can talk to her about it and start speaking up in meetings and sharing your accomplishments more frequently.
- If someone constantly asks for you to take on their work for them, you can set boundaries so you can keep up with your own responsibilities. Explain that you are happy to offer advice and guidance, but that you have a heavy workload.

There is almost always something you can do to decrease your stress. Ask yourself what steps you can take to make things better.

OVERCOME IMPOSTOR SYNDROME

"I don't know how to do this project and everyone else is going to know." "I don't deserve this job." "I would volunteer for that high-profile project, but everyone else on the team has done it before, and I won't be as good at it."

Sound familiar? If so, you may be experiencing impostor syndrome, which is another common source of stress in the workplace, especially for new employees. People who are smart and talented, yet feel insecure and uncapable, often face this challenge. You don't think you are as competent as people think you are—and you worry that people are going to realize that and think you are an "impostor" or "fraud." First studied in the late 1970s by psychologists Suzanne Imes and Pauline Rose Clance, impostor syndrome usually strikes high achievers who feel inadequate, are hard on themselves, and feel an overwhelming pressure to be perfect. It can sap your self-confidence and lead to the bad habit of ignoring your accomplishments in favor of wallowing over your mistakes. It's a major source of stress and can keep you from taking on the challenging projects that help you get ahead. The good news is that you can overcome impostor syndrome and start feeling more confident ASAP.

Give Yourself a Reality Check

Remind yourself that your perception is not a fact. When you feel self-conscious, anxious, or inadequate, you're more likely to continue to see everything at work through that lens. When you're focusing on these feelings, you're more likely to make incorrect assumptions and blow things out of proportion. Try these ideas:

- Push away nagging negative thoughts by reminding yourself that you were hired for this job because you are smart, talented, and motivated.
- Acknowledge and celebrate your accomplishments and remember that it was your hard work—not luck—that brought them about.
- At the end of every workday or once a week, write down three things you are proud of and a list of the most important things you did that day. Start each sentence with "I did" or "I'm proud that I" so you practice attributing your success to your actions.
- If you feel comfortable, confide in a trusted coworker you're close with to see if her perception of the situation aligns with your own.

If you're struggling with these thoughts frequently and you notice that you're self-sabotaging, make an appointment with a therapist to find out if there is a more serious issue like anxiety or depression and identify coping mechanisms.

Remember That Failing Doesn't Mean You're a Failure

When you're already feeling low, every mistake can feel like a bigger deal than it is. You should always strive to be careful, prepared, and organized, but everyone messes up occasionally. If you beat yourself up over every error, you may actually be more prone to making mistakes. It's hard to think clearly when you're preoccupied and anxious.

Try to remember that making a mistake, or even totally failing at a task, does not mean you are a failure. Learn from your mistakes and move on. You could say a mantra like "The only mistakes are things you don't learn from," "You learn more from failure than success," or "Everyone makes mistakes. Shake it off." When you get that sinking feeling in your stomach when you realize you've messed up, take a few minutes to calm down. Go for a walk around the block; do a five-minute guided meditation; or try a breathing exercise like closing your eyes and taking a few deep breaths, imagining you are breathing in calm and confidence, releasing stress and self-doubt. Get your journal and note a few things you could do differently next time. If this happens continually, write down how your goal for perfection is holding you back. It might take longer to complete projects, make you hard on yourself and others, and keep you from taking on challenging work because you worry you won't be able to do it "perfectly." When you struggle with perfectionism, you often are more critical of yourself and are prone to negative self-talk, like thinking that you aren't good enough or fixating on your mistakes.

Set Realistic Goals and Celebrate When You Reach Them

When you have feelings of impostor syndrome, it can be hard to recognize and acknowledge your accomplishments. You tend to downplay your successes by attributing them to "luck" or other external factors. Setting realistic goals and breaking apart big goals into smaller, more immediately attainable ones will give you opportunities to celebrate your achievements and increase your self-esteem.

HANDLE NEGATIVE FEEDBACK

No one likes to hear what they've done wrong, what they're not good at, or where they need to improve, but these conversations can lead to positive change. Still, they can be stressful. By listening to the constructive criticism, interpreting it correctly, and acting on the feedback, you can handle a bad review or uncomfortable conversation, implement the advice and, ultimately, improve the quality of your work.

Moderate Your Initial Reaction

The first thing to do is not panic. If your boss is talking to you in person, take a deep breath. If the feedback came in an email, go for a walk to calm down. Getting angry or defensive will make it harder to take in the feedback. It will make it less likely that people will provide constructive criticism in the future.

The benefit of getting this type of feedback in an email is that you can take time to collect your thoughts and you don't have to respond immediately. The tough thing is that it's harder to interpret someone's tone and equally tough to convey your own, so what you type can be misinterpreted. You can simply say "Thanks for your feedback. Would you have a few minutes to talk about this in person? Please let me know a convenient time for you." That gives you time to compose your thoughts while avoiding any possible misunderstanding.

You don't have the liberty of a delayed reaction when you're speaking in person, but you can pause to take a deep breath and think about what you're going to say before you start talking. Emotions can run high in difficult situations like these, and collecting your thoughts will help you think of what to say. If you still feel very upset, say you'd like to collect your thoughts before continuing the conversation.

Listen Carefully

As the person gives you the feedback, listen closely to what they're saying and show that you've acknowledged it. Try repeating what they said back to them in your own words, as in "You're saying that I've missed a few important deadlines." This lets the person know that they're being heard and will help you remember the feedback in the future. If you have a notebook with you, take notes during the conversation so you can look back at them later.

Although you don't want to seem defensive, it is okay to explain your perspective so your boss can step in with suggestions. If you're having trouble meeting deadlines because you feel like you're juggling too many projects, tell her. Ask questions so you completely understand what went wrong and what you need to improve. You can use this time to problem-solve together and fix what went wrong before it gets any worse.

Take Time to Reflect

Once you've heard the feedback and gone back to work, try your best not to take the feedback personally or blow it out of proportion. Listen to feedback objectively and realize that it's not a reflection on your personal attributes but rather is simply a recommendation for how you can improve at work.

Write out some of the main points from the conversation and, if relevant, action items you can take moving forward. And, as much as you'd probably like to move on and never think about it again, check your notes in a few weeks to make sure you stay accountable. Schedule a time to follow up with the person who gave you the feedback and go over your improvements. That way they know you've worked to improve your performance and that you took what they said to heart.

USE YOUR COMPANY'S BENEFITS TO YOUR ADVANTAGE

That folder or website with information about benefits that the human resources department gave you on your first day usually contains some really valuable tools for decreasing stress in many aspects of your life.

Health Insurance

One of the best examples of a benefit that can help you feel less stressed is having health insurance. Without it, you could be stuck with sky-high medical bills if you get sick or hurt. Health insurance gives you peace of mind to know that you are covered in case of an emergency or a higher-than-expected annual checkup bill.

It isn't mandatory for all US companies to offer health insurance to full-time employees, but most do so they can recruit the best talent. In exchange for a monthly fee known as a premium, insurance companies pay part of your medical bills. When a company offers health insurance, the employer pays all or part of your premium. They may cover all or part of your premium for partner and children, once you're ready for that.

Most plans offer tiers of benefits, so read the fine print to choose one that works best for you based on your health needs. You can search most health insurance companies' websites to find in-network doctors (ones that take your insurance). With an in-network doctor, you might only have a copay, or you might have a copay once you hit your deductible, depending on your plan. Some plans will pay for you to go to an out-of-network doctor, usually after you hit your deductible, but some require you to pay the full bill. You'll need to submit a claim after each doctor's appointment before you get reimbursed. If you go to a doctor that takes insurance, they will usually fill out and submit the claim for you. If you go to a doctor that doesn't take insurance, you may have to go online to your healthcare provider to fill out the form. Your plan's benefits may include dental, vision, and disability insurance. If you are younger than twenty-six and a US citizen, you can stay on your parents' plan if they have one. (In some instances, you can get an extension.)

- **Coinsurance:** The percentage of costs of a covered health care service that you pay.
- **Copayment:** A fixed amount you pay for a covered health care service.
- **Deductible:** The amount you need to pay before your insurance provider starts to pay.
- **Out-of-pocket maximum:** The most you have to pay for covered health care services in a year. Once you spend this amount on your deductible, copayments, and coinsurance, your health care provider will start to pay 100 percent of the costs of covered benefits. (Some plans will offer copays before you hit your deductible.)

Many companies offer an Employee Assistance Program (EAP), which gives you access to a set number of confidential sessions with a counselor who can help with stress, depression, grief, financial stress, and other personal issues and work-related problems like anxiety at work. A counselor can recommend other therapists or resources.

— TO DO —
TRACK YOUR MEDICAL EXPENSES

Signing up for health insurance and paying your own medical bills might be completely new to you. Try not to be overwhelmed by the statements and bills; instead, use this worksheet to track things yourself. Accounting for all of your medical expenses will help you know if you paid your bills, how much you paid, and if you've been reimbursed by your health insurance provider.

Appointment Date	Doctor	Description of Visit	Amount Paid and Date	Date Sent Claim (If You Sent It Yourself)	Reimburse-ment Amount and Date

---

Time Off

Decrease stress by taking some time off work. Strategize your paid time off so you spread it out over the calendar year. If you have some extra money, you might be able to travel, but if not, have a staycation.

Get as much of your work done as possible before you go on vacation. If someone on the team will have to cover for you, meet with them in advance.

Save a few days to use for mental health or sick days. Taking a day off now and then can help you de-stress and get some much-needed R&R so you go back to work feeling reenergized instead of burned out.

Financial Resources

For many people, money is one of the biggest sources of stress. There are many work benefits that can help you feel more financially secure—other than the excitement of payday. Take advantage of benefits like health savings accounts (HSA) or flexible spending accounts (FSA), 401(k) matching, and perks your company offers like discounts on gym memberships, insurance, or cell phone plans. These plans can help you save money.

DEAL WITH MAJOR WORKPLACE ISSUES

Sometimes more serious issues can come up at the office that can create short- or long-term stress in your life. Discrimination, harassment, and extended illnesses are unfortunate realities. Hopefully you will not have to deal with them in your career, but if you do, there are procedures and people who can help.

Extended Medical Leave

You may need to take time off or need other accommodations for health reasons. In the US, you have protection under laws like the Americans with Disabilities Act (ADA) and the Family and Medical Leave Act (FMLA), should you need them. You can take time off for parental leave, to take care of a sick family member, or for your own serious health issue. For more information about your protections, check out the US Equal Employment Opportunity Commission (EEOC) at www.eeoc.gov.

Discrimination and Harassment

In the US, Title VII of the Civil Rights Act of 1964 prohibits employers from discriminating on the basis of sex, race, color, national origin, and religion. The law protects against illegal harassment that makes the workplace intimidating, hostile, or abusive. The EEOC investigates workplace harassment and discrimination in the US.

Visit their website www.eeoc.gov for more information on what to do if you feel you are being harassed. You have a right to report harassment, participate in a harassment investigation or lawsuit, or oppose harassment without being retaliated against.

No job should ever make you feel depressed, anxious, bullied, overworked, or diminished. It's vital to know your rights and how to report a problem…or get out of a toxic workplace.

DECIDE IF IT IS TIME TO MOVE ON

Is the best part of your workday your drive home? Do you dream about walking out that door and never returning? If so, it's probably time to start looking for a new position.

If You're Unhappy in Your Position

If there is something reasonable that you could do or ask for to make your job more rewarding, ask. Meet with your manager to see if she can help. If you're overwhelmed with your workload and consistently work late to get everything done, she might be able to help you prioritize, give some of your work to another coworker, or suggest how you might be more efficient.

That meeting is the time to tell her if you'd like a different challenge at work. If you like the company but not your particular position, don't quit just yet. It's always better to ask and see if anything else is available. The worst your boss can say is no.

If You're Not Learning New Skills

If you've proactively sought out new projects or more responsibilities and you still aren't feeling challenged, it might be time to find something new. Learning new things and improving your skills help you advance in your career and keep you from getting bored. Try looking for jobs that are similar enough to your own so that you know you'll succeed but that are different enough that you'll get a new spark of energy from the change.

There's No Room for Advancement

If you don't have a clear path for promotions and growth at your company, either because people can't get promoted until someone leaves a position or because you keep getting passed up, it's time to spruce up your resume and cover letter.

If you aren't getting raises, either because your boss doesn't think you've earned them or there are budget issues, research the market rate for your role and how much you'd get paid at a different company. Websites like *Glassdoor* and *PayScale* can give you an average range for your industry. Sometimes the only way to make a big salary jump is to move to another company with higher salaries or to take advantage of a new opportunity to negotiate your salary.

If You're Bored

If you find yourself staring at the clock every five minutes and taking tons of breaks to read articles, scroll through *Instagram*, or watch cute puppy videos on *YouTube*, you are bored at work. It's normal to need short breaks or procrastinate before beginning a new assignment, but if you are constantly bored, it might be time to find a new job. It could be as simple as finding a new challenge at your current job by switching to a new department, or it might involve looking for a new position at a different company. But sitting at your desk, bored and unproductive, isn't good for you or the company.

If you decide to quit, set up a meeting with your boss and let her know you've received another offer that you're going to take. Stay positive about your time at the company and offer at least two weeks' notice.

Leaving Your Job

It can be scary to leave the known (even if it's a known you know you don't like) for the unknown, but if nothing can improve your current situation, you owe it to yourself to try to find a job that makes you happier. Life is too short to work at a job you hate, or even just a job that you feel "meh" about. Unless you are miserable and your job is impacting your mental and physical health, it makes sense to start applying to jobs while you still have one. It takes the financial pressure off so you can be more selective. You can focus on finding a job you'll really like, instead of settling because your rent is due.

Points to Remember

 Ask yourself what you can do to decrease your stress at work. There is always something you can do to make things better, even if it means finding a new job.

 Many people deal with impostor syndrome at some point in their career, but there are ways you can increase your confidence.

 You can learn more about your rights as an employee at www.eeoc.gov.

 Check in periodically to think about if you are still happy, motivated, and challenged at work. If not, it might be time to start looking for something new.

Chapter 5

Strengthen Work Relationships

When you have good working relationships with your coworkers, you're likely to be happier, more productive, and less stressed. The workday goes by much faster and is more fun when you have someone to chat with, get advice from (and vice versa), and sit with at lunch. You need a support system at work just as much as you need one in your personal life. It's so beneficial to have people who encourage you, motivate you, and make you more successful by helping with projects, giving advice, and speaking highly of you to peers and higher-ups.

Besides friends, you'll have other coworkers alongside you, such as a mentor and sponsor and your boss. There is a lot of research that backs up the simple fact that strong work relationships increase job satisfaction and can lead to promotions and raises and reaching your goals faster because you prioritize collaboration over competition.

If you follow the advice in this chapter, you'll have two of the most important keys to career success: a strong work ethic and a strong support system at work.

UNDERSTAND THE COMPANY CULTURE

Company culture describes how people work together and the behaviors, values, and goals that are promoted and rewarded at the company.

Many companies have a set list of company values they want everyone on the team to embody. Some organizations are hierarchical and formal, like a corporate law firm or large consulting firm, while others are flat and informal, like many startups. You'll get a feel for the company culture by getting to know people at all levels of the organization and learning more about the leadership team. When you're new and need a quick rundown, many companies have their corporate values, mission, and goals stated right on their Careers or About pages.

Learn the Rules of the Game

Every office has unwritten rules. Watch how your boss or people who have been with the company a while do things. What behavior is rewarded or penalized? Observe everything, including the time people get in and leave work, whether they offer constructive criticism in meetings, if they always go to office events, and if they get together with coworkers after hours.

Recognizing and following your office's unwritten rules is a key to getting ahead. Your employee handbook won't say whom you should befriend at work because their opinion matters or how late you are *actually* expected to stay. Working hard and doing a good job are certainly crucial, but if you want to get ahead, you have to understand what gets people promoted and how to get along with your coworkers. (Of course, if there are any unwritten rules that are unethical or illegal or that make you uncomfortable like overstating numbers in new business pitches or people doing drugs at work or work events, it is time to start looking for a new job.)

Get the Right People in Your Corner

People who get ahead at work don't do it alone; they have a strong support network. It can seem opportunistic to consciously plan to forge strong working relationships with the "right" people, but that's a key part of office politics. So, who should be on the top of your list? Your boss, peers on the "fast track," a mentor, and a sponsor.

Your boss's feedback matters the most when it comes time for reviews, raises, and promotions. She's the person who works most closely with you and knows the most about your performance. She has to like the quality of your work *and* working with you, so make sure you maintain a good relationship with her and keep her happy.

Peers on the "fast track" are clearly doing something right. Befriend them and learn what they're doing that's helping them succeed. There's a good chance they are not just good at their jobs but also have strong relationships at work and understand the unwritten rules of the office. Seek out high performers throughout the company to get a clear understanding of the goals and priorities across the organization.

You can have mentors outside of your office, like a college professor or someone you meet at an industry event, but it is also helpful to have a mentor in your office to help you work through any problems you might have. Choose someone who understands the company culture and the people in your department you refer to when you ask for advice. Your mentor could be someone who has the position you'd like to have in the future, your boss, or a peer who has been at the company longer than you. Find someone you trust and admire and learn from them.

A sponsor is different than a mentor. A mentor gives you advice that will help you advance at work; a sponsor advocates for you. A sponsor, similar to a mentor, can give you advice, but she will help you get the opportunities you need to get ahead at work. She'll request that you get a spot on a high-profile project or are invited to important meetings. She will speak highly of you to the people who decide on promotions and raises. You can have someone who is both a mentor and a sponsor if the person works in your office and can either get you the next promotion or big assignment or advocate for you and influence the decision-makers.

The best way to find a sponsor is to do great work and establish strong relationships with people higher than you on the office hierarchy so they will feel invested in your career and use their access and influence over decision-makers to open doors for you.

CULTIVATING A GREAT RELATIONSHIP WITH YOUR BOSS

Your most important work relationship is with your boss, in part because you work most closely together and in part because their feedback matters the most when it comes to performance evaluations, raises, and promotions.

Just how important is your relationship with your boss? Surveys have shown that when people feel supported by their boss they feel valued, motivated to do their best work, and are happier at work. How do you develop a strong and supportive working relationship with your boss? These tips will help.

Get Crystal Clear on Expectations

It's hard to meet or exceed your boss's expectations if you don't know what she's looking for—so ask. If you know exactly what your boss expects from you, you can focus on doing those things to the best of your ability. You could ask her to list the exact responsibilities of your role, to outline what the key metrics are, and to explain how she defines success for your role.

Once you have the answers, make an action plan that you can use to work toward those goals. Remember that priorities and responsibilities shift periodically, so make it a habit to check in with your boss for a similar conversation at least once a quarter. Do the same thing on a smaller scale by asking about your responsibilities and goals for every project before you start. As you learn more about what your boss expects of you, you can begin to anticipate her needs and solve her problems before she even knows they exist.

Write down all the constructive feedback you get and be sure to implement it. Keep track of positive feedback so you know what to continue.

Some managers will give you feedback seemingly 24/7, some save it until your annual review, and some might even keep all their opinions to themselves. Check in with your boss at least once a quarter to talk about your strengths, weaknesses, and areas for improvement. You don't need a formal review or conversation to ask for feedback.

Learn Your Manager's Preferences

You don't have to go as far as knowing that your boss drinks venti almond milk lattes, but you should know her work preferences. You can ask her directly or simply observe the little nuances in her behavior. Does she respond more favorably when you stop by her office when you have a question, or should you shoot her an email? If she sends an email on the weekend, does she expect a response right away or is she just bored at her kid's soccer game and everything can wait for Monday? How does she like your reports filed: digitally or on paper?

Be Accountable

The best and simplest way to make your boss happy is to do your job well. If you say you are going to do something, such as meeting a tight deadline or sending out the agenda for a meeting, do it. It keeps everyone happy and shows that you're on top of your work. If there ever comes a time that you can't follow through for some reason, your boss will be much more understanding if it's something that rarely happens.

GET ALONG WITH YOUR COWORKERS

You spend at least forty hours a week with your coworkers. These aren't just the people you'll sit next to in meetings, laugh with while making coffee, and work with on projects; they are the people who will give you advice, guidance, and helpful feedback, and they can help teach you the skills you need to move forward in your career. In fact, 2018 research from Gallup showed that having a best friend at work leads people to do better work, feel more engaged and motivated, take more risks that lead to innovation, and feel connected to their coworkers. They are more likely to feel happy and recognized for their work and less likely to feel anxious, stressed, or tired. You don't have to be best friends with everyone in the office, but being friendly, reliable, and collaborative is good for your mental health and your career.

Respect People's Time

Respecting people's time is about more than showing up to meetings on time. Show up prepared. Try your best to anticipate feedback, questions, and next steps on assignments so you don't waste time searching for the answer. Ask relevant questions to make sure you are doing something correctly so no one has to spend time fixing a mistake. (But think before you ask a question and don't ask ones that can be found in a five-second Google search.) Respond to emails or calls promptly. If a coworker seems overwhelmed and you have extra time, ask if there is anything you can do to help. Make sure you need a meeting rather than an email.

Be Collaborative

Don't just focus on your own priorities and accomplishing your goals. Working together as a team helps the entire company thrive. Share your skills and expertise with your coworkers, whether it's something small, like helping them fix a printer jam, or something big, like staying late to help finish an urgent project.

Some industries thrive on competition, but you should never undermine your coworkers by stealing their ideas, taking credit for their work, or purposely leaving them out of an important meeting. Being collaborative and helping out your coworkers is the right thing to do; it helps everyone do a better job. Plus, when you need some support, your colleagues will want to help you in return.

Show Appreciation

The simplest way to show appreciation is to say "Thank you." But don't just say a quick "thanks" at the end of an email—be specific and explain why someone's action was helpful and the impact it made. It shows that you used their help and that their contribution made a difference. Likewise, when someone has a big accomplishment such as landing a client or getting a promotion, give your congratulations.

Small gestures like these can go a long way in building strong, lasting relationships, ones that will make your work experience much better. It helps to build strong work relationships because it shows that you notice other people's achievements and that you are supportive and encouraging rather than viewing someone else's success as a threat to your own.

MASTER THE UNWRITTEN RULES OF WORK FRIENDSHIPS

You likely spend more time with your coworkers than your friends and family each week. If you get along with them, all the better. You might have one or two close work friends that you like to get together with outside of work at happy hours, workouts, or just to watch Netflix, and you might have some work friends that you are only friends with "in the office." No matter how close you are with them, you need to maintain boundaries with work friends to make sure your working relationships stay positive.

Think Before You Overshare

You might want to tell your nonwork friends everything, but you need to have boundaries and filters with your work friends that aren't necessary with your best friends from high school or college.

Be mindful what you share because there's no way to make sure it will remain a secret. Your friend might share what you said with other people in the office, and that could affect your job or reputation. Let's say you told a work friend that you made a huge mistake that could cause problems for the company. Even though you asked her not to tell anyone, she may feel like she has to if a manager asks about the situation or if there may be a way to fix it.

Don't share anything that you wouldn't want the CEO to know. Remember that everything you say over email, instant messenger, or text message can be screenshot or forwarded. The bottom line: Be mindful of what you share.

Respect the Hierarchy

Even in laid-back offices with a relaxed corporate culture, your boss is your boss. Your relationships with your boss or anyone else above you on the company hierarchy have to be treated with more discretion than your friendships with peers in the office. You can be friendly with your boss, but be careful of how it affects your professional relationship and how it might be perceived by coworkers. If you hang out on weekends and have lots of inside jokes, it could be seen as favoritism, even if it's not.

Resolve Disagreements Professionally

Given that you spend so much time together, it's natural that you might get on a coworker's nerves sometimes and vice versa. Don't let a personal disagreement mess up your professional relationship—talk about it and make up as quickly and maturely as possible to avoid causing rifts in the workplace. The way to resolve a disagreement with a work friend is the same as resolving one with your other friends, family members, or your partner: You should both calm down before you talk about the issue so you don't say anything you regret. When you're ready to talk, listen and try to understand the other person's perspective, and explain your own without pointing fingers. You might need to admit that you were wrong or find a compromise. Look for ways to avoid the same disagreement in the future, then try to move forward without harping on it.

Don't Form Cliques

It's normal to get along better with some people at work than others, but be careful not to give off the vibe that your friend group is an exclusive clique. No one likes to be excluded, and it could lead to people treating you differently because they think you are snobby or aloof…even though you're not. Include other people in the conversation and introduce coworkers who might not know each other.

Be Careful about Dating

Many offices have employee dating policies that require you to disclose your relationship to human resources (and you thought becoming "*Instagram* official" was a big deal!) or require one of you to transfer to another team.

Before you start a relationship with a coworker, make sure the feeling is mutual and that anything that happens is absolutely consensual, which should be your standard anyway. Some companies have explicit rules prohibiting dating someone who is above or below you in the company hierarchy or someone who works in the same department as you--and for good reason. When you date someone on a different level of the organization, one person may feel pressured into the relationship or fear what would happen if they say no. There may be a concern that it might create an unfair advantage in the workplace, with the person in the relationship getting more favorable assignments and better reviews regardless of actual performance. The power dynamics involved with dating your boss or someone you manage can be a tricky situation—one that's best avoided.

If you do decide to date a coworker, make sure to limit any PDA in the office and keep work conversations appropriate to the workplace. If it doesn't work out and you break up, make sure you can still work well together and that you are professional.

NETWORK WITH COLLEAGUES

Keep track of your professional connections using *LinkedIn, Twitter,* and *Instagram.* You never know when a contact could help you find a new job, introduce you to a new client, or give you valuable career advice. And *you* might be able to do any of these things for people you know.

Follow People You Admire

First, begin connecting with and following people in your current or intended industry, such as coworkers, clients, and mentors. You can connect with people who have similar career interests (say, if you are both members of the same professional group) or side jobs (for example, if you are a nurse and have a photography business).

Get inspiration for growing your own social media following by asking yourself:

- What articles do they read and recommend?
- Do they share industry tips? How?
- Do they share personal *and* professional content and if so, what's the balance?
- Which hashtags do they use?

Take notes for your own posts.

Interact with People

Once you've gotten a sense of how people you admire operate, reach out.

- Respond to people's posts with thoughtful comments, or ask follow-up questions.
- Congratulate your connections on their accomplishments.
- Post an article you think your followers might enjoy.
- Instead of asking for general advice like "tips for freelance writers," ask if you could read one of her article pitches or what job search sites she recommends for finding a job in your industry.

Don't ask anything you could find out from a quick Google search because she has already written or spoken about it.

Before you post something, think about whether you should reach out to your whole network, a small group, or a single person. Above all, be considerate and genuine and try to get to know people.

Once you've gathered a number of personal and professional contacts, from professors to former coworkers to people you've met at networking events, reach out to people frequently, even if it is just "liking" or commenting on their posts. If you are interacting with them more regularly on social media, you can keep the conversation going all the time, not just when you have a favor to ask.

Ask for a Favor

You might want to reach out to someone with a specific request—such as an introduction to someone they know, advice on your career path, or a recommendation for a job. In those cases, send a short, direct message on social media or an email with a brief introduction and your "ask." If you have a quick question, you can ask on social media, but if it is a longer question that would be tough to type out on a phone or you are trying to make plans, it's easier to switch to email. It's helpful if you've already interacted with the person on social media first so they are familiar with you before you ask for a favor.

Ask for something reasonable. You might see if they have time for a short phone call, if they could meet up for coffee, or if you could email them a few questions. (Hint: Most companies have formulas for their email addresses like firstname.lastname@companyname.com or firstinitial.lastname@companyname.com. Do some sleuthing because if you can find one person's email address, you can usually find them all!)

──────── TO DO ────────
WRITE A MESSAGE TO SOMEONE YOU HAVEN'T MET

Even if you've connected with people on social media, you might not know them well. If you'd like to reach out to someone, write your note in a clear, professional way to present yourself well and increase the likelihood that you'll hear back. Follow these steps:

1. Write a specific subject line that explains something you have in common, a mutual connection, or something you admire that is leading you to reach out like "Learning about Your Columbia Journalism School Experience."

2. In the first sentence, briefly introduce yourself. If you have a mutual connection (such as the same alma mater or a shared colleague or friend), mention it in the second sentence to get the reader's attention.

3. Next, mention specifically why you're reaching out; for example, you are applying to graduate school and would like to learn about her experience with the program because it is your top choice.

4. Make your "ask" something that is easy to say yes to and include options that show that you want to be mindful of the person's time. You could ask if she has time for a five-minute phone call to discuss her experience or if you could send a few specific questions by email.

5. Use a professional sign-off such as "Best" or "All the best."

6. Read the email again for typos, spelling, grammar, and accuracy. (Make sure you spelled the person's name and company name correctly, for example.)

7. It's bothersome to get emails saying "Did you get my email?" or "Just following up." After a week with no response, you could send one follow-up email, but don't continue to check in repeatedly or switch to another communication channel like direct messaging her on *Instagram* because that can feel invasive. If she doesn't respond, try not to take it personally and move on to asking someone else for advice.

Points to Remember

- When you have strong relationships with your coworkers, you are more likely to be happier, more productive, and less stressed.

- Work is more enjoyable if you have a few close work friends. Just keep the unwritten rules of workplace friendships in mind as you forge these relationships.

- Try to establish strong working relationships with your boss, peers on the "fast track," a mentor, a sponsor, and a few close work friends.

- Stay in touch with your existing network and reach out to new people to learn from them.

Chapter 6

How to Get Promoted

After you've been in your job for a while, you might be ready for a new challenge. Your five-year-plan goals might even be pushing you to move ahead. In this chapter, you'll learn how to show you're ready for more responsibility, set and meet your goals, develop your strengths and weaknesses, and become an effective manager.

EXCEED EXPECTATIONS

Once you are confident about your ability to handle your day-to-day responsibilities, start thinking of ways you can do more than what's asked of you. Think of a problem no one else in your department wants to handle, like a project that needs more attention or a complicated task that could help your boss meet key goals. Prepare a plan to solve the problem and pitch it to your boss. Taking on a difficult task like this will show her that you're proactive and a problem-solver, two important characteristics of success. Always think about what you can do to make a positive impact on the company's bottom line.

At the end of the day, businesses exist to make money, and you'll be seen as more valuable and more of a leader if you understand and accomplish the business's key objectives.

Talk to your boss as well. Your boss isn't a mind reader and has her own goals and objectives to meet. She might not realize that you *want* to take on more responsibilities, lead projects, and eventually get promoted. Set up a short meeting to talk to your boss about your goals, ask for feedback, and find out specific skills you need to focus on to be on track for a promotion.

DEVELOP YOUR STRENGTHS AND MINIMIZE YOUR WEAKNESSES

Another way to move forward with your career trajectory is to focus on what you do best. It's hard to be really great at things you don't enjoy, and people don't usually enjoy doing the things they aren't great at. That doesn't mean you shouldn't take assignments that challenge you or that you'll find a job that magically requires only your strongest skills; it just means that, on balance, you should look for projects that require more of your strengths than your weaknesses.

If you are having trouble identifying your strengths, try this exercise developed by researchers at University of Michigan's Center for Positive Organizations:

1. Identify ten people from your professional and personal life who know you well, such as friends, family, professors, mentors, and current and past coworkers. Email each person and ask them to share what they think are your five top strengths as well as a specific story about when they saw your strengths in action.

2. Once you get everyone's feedback, analyze it to find the common themes. Make a list of the themes, the examples given, and what you think the feedback suggests about what you do well and the type of projects in which you'll excel.

3. Write out two to four paragraphs about who you are when you are at your best. In doing this, you'll be able to clearly see your strengths and the type of work you do best.

4. The next step is to adapt based on what you've identified by finding ways to play to your strengths more in your current role so you show your value and get promoted sooner. Let's say your first sentence is "I perform my best when I am writing content that helps people feel more confident in their personal and professional lives." You have identified that your top skill is writing actionable content. If you work at a news publication, for example, you can start pitching ideas that fit this new beat so you're writing about the topics that interest you most and using your strongest skill.

TRACK AND SHARE YOUR ACCOMPLISHMENTS

There's a time to be humble when you achieve success…but there's a time to let people know how well you're doing! In an ideal world, your coworkers would recognize all of your achievements automatically (and there would be office puppies, free catered meals, and unlimited vacation days). But in most workplaces, it's your responsibility to share your accomplishments with people.

Keep a Wins Folder

Make an email folder or one on your desktop to store positive emails from coworkers and clients. Add in anything you worked on that you are especially proud of, such as a successful presentation or a pitch for an idea that helped the company. Keeping everything in one spot makes it easy to find when you need it for your review or when you ask for your next promotion. Plus, it's a nice pick-me-up when you're having a bad day!

RECORD YOUR ACCOMPLISHMENTS AT WORK

Take a few minutes each week to reflect and plan ahead. Answer these questions in your journal so you have a record of feedback and accomplishments ready when you ask for a promotion.

1. What are the top three things I accomplished this week?

_____

_____

_____

2. What feedback did I get this week?

_____

_____

_____

3. What could I have done better this week?

_____

_____

_____

4. What are the top three things I want to accomplish next week?

_____

_____

_____

5. What are action items for accomplishing next week's goals?

_____

_____

_____

Tell the World about Your Wins

If you worked hard on a project and did a great job, take credit for that and let people know about your accomplishments. When you have major successes like winning a case, getting press, or being honored with an award, mention it on social media, including *LinkedIn*, to let your professional support network know.

Letting higher-ups know that you're doing well in your job will put you on their radar the next time promotions come around. Some people get uncomfortable sharing their success because they don't want to sound like they are bragging, but it is critical to getting ahead at work. People are so busy with their own overflowing inboxes and to-do lists that they might not notice all the great work you are doing. If it was a team effort, explain how the team was able to accomplish the goal and point out any key team members who made it a success. Phrasing it this way will make you and your teammates feel good—everyone likes recognition for hard work. There will be certain things that you are solely responsible for—in this case, get comfortable giving yourself credit for a job well done by sharing with your friends and family first. Another way to get more comfortable is to share things that are quantifiable, like the number of sales you made and the impact it had on the business.

You don't have to limit it to just VIPs in your company, either. Email mentors, former coworkers you've stayed in touch with, and other friends in the industry. They want to know about your accomplishments, and it will help you keep up the conversation with your network.

No one cares about your career more than you do, so you have to advocate for yourself. Get used to talking about your accomplishments without downplaying them.

ASK FOR A PROMOTION

Some companies only give out raises and promotions once a year at annual reviews, but by that time executives have probably already decided on the budget and whom to promote, so it's in your best interest to operate on a different timeline. Follow these steps:

1. **Talk to your boss six months before your annual review to share that you'd like to be considered for a promotion.** (If you just started working, wait until the end of your first year to start asking for promotions so you can prove yourself first.) Ask for specific feedback about what you are doing well, what you can improve on, and the skills you'll need to land the promotion. By being proactive, you'll have ample time to develop your strengths and weaknesses and start taking on more responsibilities so you can show that you deserve a promotion.

2. **Make a list of your top accomplishments.** Prioritize any accomplishments that make the company money, are quantifiable, and show that you are already taking on the skills necessary for the next role. You'll use those as talking points when you ask for a promotion at your annual review.

3. **Determine your goal salary.** Raises are usually given out at annual reviews, and, if you are promoted, the new role will hopefully come with a significantly bigger paycheck. If you are close with coworkers at the next level, ask if they are comfortable sharing how much they make, and check sites like *PayScale* or Salary.com. Now you'll have a baseline number in mind when you start to negotiate.

4. Think about what you want to say. Before your annual review, practice the conversation with a friend, family member, partner, or mentor and have them ask you questions so you can think of your answers in advance. It is possible that you won't get a raise or promotion because there isn't enough room in the budget, there isn't a role available, or the decision-makers don't think you are ready for it yet. You can ask for other things like professional development opportunities or if you can revisit the conversation sooner than your next annual review and find out exactly what you'll need to do to get ahead.

Points to Remember

 Exceed your job responsibilities to show you are ready for more challenging work.

 If you're not sure which direction to go next, focus on your strengths. If you're not sure what your strengths are, ask trusted people for suggestions.

 Keep track of your accomplishments weekly. When it comes time to make a case for your promotion, you'll have lots of proof.

Part 2

FINANCES

Make it enjoyable to take control of your financial future by having clear goals, action items, and manageable steps that leave you feeling empowered and excited, not overwhelmed. The goals you wrote in Chapter 1 should lead the way—let them keep you motivated to continue learning and making progress.

Chapter 7
Master Money Basics

When you're learning about money, start with the financial skills that you'll need to reach your goals. Simple things like creating an emergency fund or budgeting create good habits that will last a lifetime. Being strategic about your money will help you build your confidence—and your credit score.

In this chapter, you'll learn skills to help you use your money wisely. Planning financial goals, paying down your debt, and finding apps to help you manage everything will help you prepare for the future and plan for big purchases like a car or house. Creating smart spending and saving habits will help you throughout your life.

UNDERSTAND THE BENEFITS OF BUDGETING

A budget is a spending plan that you make based on your income and expenses. You look at your income for a set amount of time, like a month, and decide how you'll allocate your money. A good budget shouldn't be a hassle—it should make you feel excited and empowered. You'll have better control over your finances, so you'll know when you're free to buy that new jacket you saw and when you have to save that money to pay off your student loan debt.

A budget takes into account your expected income and expenses for a month so you can see your spending patterns, plan for your monthly needs and wants, and make progress toward your longer-term goals. And it's really easy to create a comprehensive and easy-to-follow budget!

There are many reasons that making a budget is worth some effort.

It Opens Your Eyes to Your Spending

Budgeting helps you see exactly how you're spending your money—something you may not actually be aware of. You might not realize how much small expenses like $10 salads, $4.50 lattes, $15 movie theater tickets, and Uber trips add up. It can seem like small purchases are just that, small purchases, but when you see the grand total that you could save and what you could put it toward instead, making your own lunch or coffee may seem like the better option.

It's Easier to Reach Your Goals

When you plan your budget in advance, you can make sure you are spending and saving money strategically so you can hit the financial goals you set in your five-year plan. You might have things you want in the moment like new clothes and shoes, dinners out, or a new TV. However, if you buy those things without thinking ahead, you're thinking in the moment instead of planning for the future, and planning is what it takes to save up for milestones like paying off your student loans, buying a car, or purchasing a home.

It Helps You Save Money

Budgeting can help you identify ways to save money. Maybe you can opt to eat out only on weekends, to pack lunch every day instead of buying overpriced salads, or to use a fitness app instead of paying for an expensive gym membership.

REVIEW YOUR GOALS

Review the goals you wrote down in Chapter 1. Make sure they covered all of your goals, no matter how big or small. Once you have the entire list, organize it by what's most important. Your top priorities should be big, repeating expenses, like paying off your student loans, cutting down your credit card debt, and saving money for rent. Now that you have everything prioritized, write down the amount you want to save for each goal and each step. For example, you may want to put $150 per month toward paying back your student loans or contributing to an emergency fund.

Be Ready for Ups and Downs

As you think about your goals, remember that your financial status will shift as your life changes—in both negative and positive ways. You might get a raise or bonus and be able to reach some of your goals faster than you thought. Maybe your priorities change as you start to plan a wedding, take a lower-paying job you love, or go back to graduate school.

You can make a budget even when you have student loans or credit card debt. You might not have a lot of leftover money, but it's still worth keeping track of what's coming in and going out so you can plan what is most important.

Your financial status isn't set in stone, but your check-ins should be. Make a standing thirty- to sixty-minute calendar appointment with yourself once a month to track your progress and prioritize any new or updated goals.

MAKE YOUR BUDGET

Now it's time to crunch the numbers. This section will explain how to make your monthly budget.

Gather Intel

To create an accurate budget, gather as many financial statements as you can, including your bank statements, credit card statements, and utility bills. Try to collect six months' to a year's worth of statements because you'll use that info to estimate your average monthly expenses.

Next, figure out your after-tax income, so you know how much money you are pocketing each month and can use that amount to plan your finances. It doesn't work to use your total salary—or pretax income—as the benchmark for your budget because it is higher than the amount you actually take home. If you use your total salary as the benchmark, it is more than you are actually earning because money is taken out for taxes and any other deductions that come out of your paycheck like your health insurance premium and 401(k) payments.

You don't have to do much math, though. Your pay stubs have a breakdown of your gross earnings and your net pay. Each pay stub should have both the current and year-to-date breakdown. Since it's a good idea to get into the habit of budgeting each month, you'll just take net income on one pay stub and multiply it by the number of times you get paid each month—usually it's biweekly, so you'd multiply by two.

Calculate All Your Monthly Expenses

Next, you need to dig through all the statements and list your monthly expenses. Be as comprehensive as possible as you follow these two steps:

1. First, write down all of your fixed costs, like car payments, auto insurance premiums, utility bills, transportation, student loan payments, and subscriptions, such as a gym membership, Wi-Fi, and cable.

2. Next, write down all of your variable costs, which change from month to month, such as groceries, dining out, seeing plays or movies, clothing shopping, buying furniture, fitness classes, or vacations. If some of your variable costs often change a lot from month to month, like if holiday shopping always makes a dent in your savings, use an average of three months.

Once you are comfortable that you've calculated all of your usual monthly expenses, knowing that it will sometimes fluctuate, subtract the total from your after-tax income. That remaining amount is the maximum you can spend each month.

Plan Out Your Goals for the Month

Now that you know how much money you have available each month, look at each of your financial goals and timelines to see if you have enough money to meet them. Based on your income and current expenses, do you have enough money left to reach your goals?

If the answer is no, take a look at all of your expenses and think of ways you can save money. Add up the savings and see if that frees up enough money for you to hit your goals.

Choose a Budgeting Technique

There are many different budgeting techniques to choose from, such as the 50/30/20 budget, the envelope system, paying yourself first, and the zero-based budget. There isn't one that's the best for everyone—the one you should use is the one you think will help you stay organized and accountable.

- **50/30/20 Budget**: This method simplifies budgeting by breaking your expenses into three categories: need-to-haves, nice-to-haves, and savings and repayment.
    - 50 percent of your income goes to things you need to have, such as rent, transportation, utilities, insurance premiums, groceries, doctor appointments, and bill payments.
    - 30 percent of your income goes to things that are nice to have, nonessential things such as a gym membership, restaurant meals, travel, and shopping.
    - 20 percent of your income goes to saving up for your medium-term and long-term goals, like your emergency fund, retirement, and paying off outstanding debt.
- **The Envelope System**: This works well if you like using cash instead of paying with a credit card. Write the name of one of your nice-to-have expenses on an envelope and put your budgeted amount inside. When it's empty, you've spent your budget for the month for that type of expense. You can use an app like Goodbudget to parcel everything out instead of using physical envelopes. You'd have to take out a lot of money to pay for your need-to-haves, savings, and debt repayment, so it's best to only use this method for your nonessentials.

- **Pay Yourself First**: This budgeting method is designed to help you pay off all of your debts and build your savings first. If you've been budgeting for a few months and don't think there is enough money left for your long-term goals like retirement and your student loans, try this method. Use the same guideline from the 50/30/20 method and set aside 20 percent for savings and debt repayment. Whatever you have left is split between things you need to have and things you'd like to have.

- **The Zero-Based Budget**: This method involves budgeting for every single dollar of your income. You'll sit down and account for all of the things you absolutely need to have, down to the penny. Once you have that planned, you can decide exactly how much money you'll spend on everything else until every dollar has a purpose.

Keep Your Budget on Track with Apps

Creating your monthly budget is the easy part—making sure you stick to it can be tougher. Keep track of your spending and saving throughout the month with a spreadsheet or app. Your budget isn't set in stone, and you'll have different priorities from month to month, like saving up for a vacation or going to a concert or play with friends.

Personal finance apps make it easier to manage your money on the go. Instead of spreadsheets and envelopes, you can use these apps that help you make a budget, check your bank account, keep track of your goals, and more.

Apps like Mint, Albert, and You Need a Budget help you organize your budget, bills, and investments. There are hundreds of personal finance apps, so find the ones that work the best for you.

If you prefer to do your own budget by hand, it will give you a more hands-on view of your finances while still giving you a complete picture of where you're at each month.

─────────────── TO DO ───────────────

FILL IN YOUR MONTHLY BUDGET WORKSHEET

Use a spreadsheet like this one to plan your budget each month and to reflect at the end of the month. This template is just to give you an idea of how you can organize your own Monthly Budget Worksheet. You can choose your own categories and expenses and keep track of it in your journal if you prefer.

Month and Year:		Yearly After-Tax Income:	
Monthly Goal:		Monthly After-Tax Income:	

Essential Expenses	Expected	Actual	Difference
Housing			
Utilities			
Groceries			
Healthcare			
Transportation			
Phone Bill			
Wi-Fi Bill			
Nonessential Expenses	**Expected**	**Actual**	**Difference**
Fitness			
Dining Out			
Travel			
Clothing			
Entertainment			

continued on next page

Savings	Expected	Actual	Difference
Retirement			
Emergency Fund			
Debt Repayment			
Monthly Totals	Expected	Actual	Difference
Total Income			
Total Expenses			
Difference			

What If Your Budget Doesn't Work Out?

The goal of a budget is for your expenses to never exceed your after-tax income. When you think your expenses may be higher than your income, look for ways you can cut back on nonessential expenses. If you've already done that, you can try to earn extra income like babysitting or picking up some shifts at your local coffee shop on weekends.

The gig economy makes it easy to earn extra income. You could find jobs like running errands, walking dogs, copyediting brochures, and setting up IKEA furniture.

You can't anticipate everything in advance. A budget is a tool to help you be more proactive, but unexpected expenses might come up, whether it is needing to buy a bridesmaid dress and plane ticket or a medical expense that you weren't anticipating. Try your best to stick to your budget because it will help you reach your financial goals, but don't be too hard on yourself if you look back and realize that you spent more than you anticipated. You can figure out ways to cover the costs the following month.

GROW YOUR EMERGENCY FUND

Once you have your priorities and goals lined up and a general budget in mind, it's time to think about some less pleasant realities, like an emergency fund. One of the first things you should start saving for is an emergency fund in case something unexpected happens, like an expensive medical bill, a home or car repair, or even losing your job. Instead of incurring debt, you'll be able to use what you've saved.

Budgeting helps you plan ahead and be proactive and so does an emergency fund. If you don't have an emergency fund, you will only plan for something like a hospital visit, expensive flights to visit a sick family member, or what you're going to do if you've just gotten laid off in the moment. When you are dealing with an emergency, the last thing you need is added stress about how you are going to pay your bills.

Try to have enough money in your emergency fund to pay for three months of expenses. You don't have to save up for an emergency fund all at once, though. Make smaller contributions each month to help you reach your target amount.

You can take some extra steps to get your emergency fund started. Try picking up some side jobs like dog walking or working weekends at a coffee shop so you won't have to touch your budget to save money.

It helps to put your emergency fund in a high-interest savings account to help it grow faster. Online banks generally have higher interest rates than traditional banks that have to pay for brick-and-mortar locations and larger teams. Some high-interest savings accounts have monthly maintenance fees or minimum balance requirements, so read the fine print to make sure the fees don't cancel out the interest. Make sure your online bank is FDIC-insured.

TACKLE YOUR DEBT

Debt grows over time, so it's in your best interest to make paying off your debt one of your biggest financial priorities. You have to pay interest on debt, so you are essentially paying a fee to borrow the money, and you need to keep paying it until you've paid off the entire loan. By paying off your debt quickly and avoiding that interest, you'll have more money for other expenses and more flexibility to make your budget work around your life. Compounding interest is great for your 401(k) and not so great for your debt, so make a plan for tackling it.

There are different strategies for paying off your debt. You can either snowball your debt or try to pay it off in an avalanche, depending on which works best for you.

- **Debt Snowball:** If you choose the debt snowball method, a term coined by finance expert Dave Ramsey, you'll pay off the smallest debt first, while simultaneously making the minimum monthly payments on the rest of your loans. You pay off your loans from smallest to largest, regardless of the interest rates. When you pay off the smallest debt, you "roll" that payment to the next smallest loan, continuing until all of your debts are paid off.

- **Debt Avalanche:** With the debt avalanche method, you prioritize based on interest rates. You'll pay off your loans with the highest interest rates first, while making your monthly minimum payments to your other loans. Once you finish paying off the loan with the highest interest rate, you take all the money you were using to pay that loan off and move it to the loan with the next-highest interest rate.

These two methods both have pros and cons. The debt snowball method gets all of the smaller loans out of the way quickly so you're not stuck making minimum payments on small loans. However, you'll be stuck paying high interest rates on your larger loans until they become your main priority. The debt avalanche method eliminates the loans with the highest interest rates first, so your debt grows less as you pay them off. The downside is that the biggest loans take longer to pay off, meaning you have to keep making minimum monthly payments on the smaller loans for a while.

It can be helpful to talk to a financial planner to get the expert advice you need to decide what option is best for you and make a plan that's customized to your financial needs and goals.

STREAMLINE YOUR FINANCIAL LIFE

When you have a long to-do list and it feels like you are juggling a million things at once, it's possible to forget about your rent bill, credit card bill, and other payments that are due. Make your life simpler by getting organized and automating as much as you can so your finances are on autopilot. You'll still need to check everything and make sure it's accurate, but you won't need to put all your bill due dates in your calendar, leave Post-it reminders on your desk, or wake up in the middle of the night because you can't remember if you paid your rent on time. You'll feel much more confident and in control if you have processes in place that make managing your money less of a chore.

Automate Your Payments

Most banks and companies will give you the option to auto-pay your bills so you don't need to keep track of all the due dates. You can automate everything from your credit card bill to your subscriptions so late payments don't end up on your credit reports and tarnish your credit score. Sign up for email notifications so you'll know when you've paid your bills. When you get the email, review all your statements to make sure everything is accurate.

Automate Your Savings

Along with auto-paying your bills, you can auto-pay yourself. You can automatically have money transferred from your checking to your savings each month, helping you grow your emergency fund. When you sign up for direct deposit of your paycheck, you can automatically have a certain percentage of every paycheck sent to your savings account.

Keep a list of all the places you set up auto-payments so it's easy to make updates if you get a new credit card.

Go Paperless

Instead of having your mailbox stuffed with bills, go paperless and get all your statements emailed to you. Not only is this more ecofriendly; you'll also be able to keep everything organized and in one place on your computer. Download the statements and bills, save them in a folder, and you'll have them all in one place if you need them. You should be able to sign up for notifications from your bank when you are getting close to incurring an overdraft fee, if you withdraw money from your bank account, or when money has been deposited into your account.

Consolidate or Eliminate Accounts

When was the last time you checked all the subscriptions you're signed up for and all the store-specific credit cards you might have signed up for to get introductory discounts? Try these three tips for reducing costs:

1. First, check all your store credit cards and make sure the perks are worth it. If all they get you is a discount, close the card and

only shop there if there's a sale. These credit cards often have high interest rates, which means you have even more bills to keep track of every month.

2. Next, check all your subscriptions to see if you can eliminate anything. A common example is to cut cable and only use streaming services like Netflix and Hulu.

3. Finally, look at your financial accounts, like credit cards, checking accounts, and savings accounts. If you have a lot of these, each with a small amount, try to consolidate them so you have less to track.

IMPROVE YOUR CREDIT SCORE

One of the benefits of streamlining your finances is that it ensures that you pay everything on time, which raises your credit score. Your credit score is a number that banks and other lenders use to decide how safe it is to lend money to you. Like a stellar Uber or Airbnb rating or a glowing recommendation letter, a great credit score will help lenders feel safer about trusting you. (You don't have just one credit score; you have a different score at each of the main credit bureaus. The most popular score measurement is a Fair Isaac Corporation model—more commonly known as a FICO score.)

Credit Scores 101

Credit scores range from 300–850, with higher numbers being better. Generally, there are five tiers for credit scores:

- **Exceptional:** 800–850
- **Very Good:** 740–799
- **Good:** 670–739
- **Fair:** 580–669
- **Very Poor:** 300–579

When you take out a loan, the lender sends your credit report—a record of your credit activity and history—to three credit bureaus: Equifax, Experian, and TransUnion. Think of it as your report card: The lenders don't necessarily all report to the same bureaus, so your credit report can differ. Each bureau will decide your credit score by weighing different factors, including whether you pay your bills on time and in full. They'll each put together a report and send it along to the lender you're working with, who will use those numbers to decide if you get the loan and the terms of the loan.

Making Sure Your Score Is Right

You have the right to get a free credit report from each bureau once a year. You can also check your credit score on a site like www.creditscore.com. Just like you check your bank account and credit card statements, make sure all the information is accurate, from your personal information like your name and address to any late or missed payments that are reported. If something isn't accurate, you can file a dispute with the credit bureau that messed up so a mistake on their end doesn't affect your ability to get a sizeable loan when you need to make a big purchase.

Raising Your Score

Five factors that affect your FICO credit score are: payment history, amount of money owed, length of credit history, new credit, and credit mix. The three that carry the most weight are payment history (your track record for paying your credit card and loan bills), amount of money owed (your current debt), and length of credit history (how long you've had your accounts).

The best way to boost your credit score is to pay your bills in full on time, to pay off your debts consistently, and to keep your credit cards open. It is likely the best way to feel confident about your finances so you can work on saving and growing your money to hit your financial goals.

Points to Remember

- Don't think about budgeting as a chore; think of it as a path to achieve your financial goals.

- Choose a budgeting system that works for you and your lifestyle, and do your best to stick to it.

- Paying off your outstanding debt should be a priority.

- Know what your credit score is, and work to improve it.

Chapter 8

Start Investing

Investing is a smart way to prepare for the future, and it doesn't require an MBA. Choosing individual stocks can be tricky, but starting with some low-cost, low-risk investments can help you build your wealth and confidence and set you up for success. In this chapter, you'll learn strategies for saving money for retirement, how to choose investment vehicles, and when to consider hiring a financial advisor. Consider this section Intro to Investing.

UNDERSTAND THE BENEFITS OF INVESTING

Investing helps you grow your money because it takes advantage of compounding, meaning that your profits start to generate profits of their own. If you leave the profits in an investment vehicle and reinvest them instead of withdrawing the money or letting it sit in a bank account, you'll continue to grow profits on the money you earn. Let's say you invest $1,000 and earn 10 percent in a year, you'll earn a profit of $100 and have $1,100 total at the end of the first year. If you reinvest that $100 and earn 10 percent in the second year, you'll make another $100 on your initial investment and $10 on the $100 profit you earned in the first year for a total of $1,210 at the end of the second year. If you continuously reinvest the profit you get, your money will likely continue to grow.

The sooner you start investing, the better off you'll be because you'll earn a return that you can reinvest to earn more. Certain types of investing are riskier than others, but you can choose the path that's right for your financial status and comfort level.

TAKE THE FIRST STEP: OPEN A BROKERAGE ACCOUNT

Think of a brokerage account like a bank account for making investments. You put money into a brokerage account at a brokerage firm and place investment orders, which the company executes for you. You can invest in stocks, bonds, and more, and you own all the assets in the account. There are some types of investments that you can buy directly from the company or the government, but a brokerage account simplifies the process and makes it easier to manage all your investments, check performance, and invest your money in a number of different areas.

There are two main types of brokerages: full-service and discount.

- A **full-service broker** will work with you directly, recommend investments, and give you financial advice; therefore, they usually charge higher fees and trading commissions.

- With a **discount broker**, you choose your investments independently, but the firm will place the orders for you. (Some will give you the option to talk to someone for a fee.) As the name suggests, discount brokers are less expensive. Some discount brokers have fees or minimum investment requirements because they are still making the investments for you, but these fees are usually much lower than if you used a full-service firm.

Do your research to compare your options and choose one that best fits your needs.

KNOW YOUR OPTIONS: STOCKS, BONDS, MUTUAL FUNDS, AND ETFS

Now it's time to learn more about the most common investment options: stocks, bonds, mutual funds, and exchange-traded funds (ETFs).

Stocks

When you buy *common stock* in a public company, you own part of the company and get to vote on important issues at the company. When they do well, you do well. If you own a stock and the company is generating a profit, it might choose to pay out a small part of that profit, called a *dividend*, to its stockholders.

You can buy *preferred stock* in a public company. Preferred stockholders give up their voting rights, but they get paid dividends before anyone else, whereas common stockholders have to wait. Preferred stock often has a higher dividend than common stock.

Warren Buffett is a famous investor known as the Oracle of Omaha thanks to his ability to invest in stocks that perform well. He recommends preferred stocks, value stocks, and investing in simple low-cost index funds as a safe way to grow your money.

You can sell your stocks at any point and make money based on your sales, but you might lose money if you buy at a certain price and then the stock price goes down. Buying individual stocks takes more strategy than other types of investing, and there is more risk involved as stock prices fluctuate based on the market.

In general, stocks are put into one of these two categories:

- **Growth stocks** are from companies whose earnings and revenues are projected to grow quickly. They are usually more expensive per share, but there is a chance for a higher growth rate.

The share prices tend to swing up and down more. These companies usually don't pay dividends yet because they are using any profits they get to invest in the business.

- **Value stocks** are from companies whose earnings and revenues are slower growing, but they usually trade at a lower price so it's less expensive to buy the stock. Value stocks normally pay dividends to shareholders.

Can't choose between value and growth? You don't have to—you can buy both.

Bonds

Bonds are loans made by a lot of people to a company or government entity. They're a fixed-income investment, meaning that they pay you back the same amount (plus interest) on a set schedule. This makes them less risky and more predictable than other types of investments, unless you invest in a company that defaults.

Unlike when you invest in stocks, fixed-rate bond payments don't change based on the market. The interest rate is fixed and you will get all of your principal (the amount you paid for the bond) unless the company defaults. You can make a profit if you sell your bond at a higher price than your purchase price. Although bonds are often less risky than stocks, they generally offer less of a return. If you buy a bond in a company that has a strong balance sheet, you are going to receive a lower interest rate but more safety than if you buy a bond in a company that doesn't have as strong a balance sheet.

Mutual Funds

When you join a mutual fund, you and a group of investors own everything in the fund, and a professional fund manager invests the collective assets. You all share the gains or losses proportionally to the amount of money you invested in the fund. Mutual funds are made up of different stocks, bonds, or a combination of both.

Mutual funds are designed and managed by a team of portfolio managers who do this for a living—meaning *you* don't have to spend a lot of time researching different stocks and bonds; they do it for you. Plus, the funds are diversified into a number of different investment categories to maximize returns and minimize risk.

Just know that if some of the investors in the mutual fund decide to sell, you will all share the "capital gains" (total money earned) and have to pay taxes on it, even if you didn't independently decide to sell.

Exchange-Traded Funds (ETFs)

Most ETFs are index ETFs, which are considered to be passive investments. The fees are lower because the person who designs the fund doesn't have to do any research. Many ETFs are designed to track a specific market index; a popular one tracks the S&P 500 Index, which measures the stock performance of 500 large US companies. ETFs are similar to mutual funds, but there are a few key differences:

- Like mutual funds, ETFs contain a collection of stocks or bonds, but they aren't designed by a fund manager like mutual funds.
- With mutual funds, you can only buy and sell at the end of the day, but ETFs trade on the stock exchange, so you can buy and sell throughout the day (so they are considered to have greater liquidity).
- Index fund ETFs are less expensive than actively managed mutual funds and *much* less expensive than hiring your own portfolio manager, and they still provide you with a diversified portfolio.

Unlike with a mutual fund, you own your "basket" individually, so you usually don't have to pay capital gains taxes unless you decide to sell your shares or collect your dividends instead of reinvesting them.

CREATE YOUR INVESTMENT STRATEGY

Now it's time to think about how you want to invest. Financial advisors recommend that you start by thinking about asset allocation.

Allocate Your Assets

Asset allocation is the process of deciding what percentage of your money is invested into the various investment options. It's a personal decision and is dependent on a combination of factors like your age and risk tolerance. Stocks are generally considered riskier than fixed-income investments like bonds or certificates of deposit (CDs), but they have the potential to generate greater returns. A CD is a savings account typically with a fixed interest rate and withdrawal date. A CD often has a higher interest rate than other savings accounts, but you have to keep your money in the account until the agreed-upon withdrawal date. Make sure the CD you choose is FDIC-insured. (Like with a lease, you can break it, but you will usually have to pay a fee.) Fixed-income investments are generally more predictable and involve less risk, but they usually generate smaller returns.

Most brokerage firms offer online questionnaires you can take to help determine your asset allocation based on your age, risk tolerance, and personal finances.

When you are younger, you can usually keep your investments in your portfolio for a long time (say, thirty or forty years). By the time you withdraw your money at the end of that period, you will probably have earned a larger return from stocks than if you invested in fixed-income investments. If you have a high risk tolerance, you might consider investing largely in stocks, because they have the potential for a greater return. If you have a low risk tolerance, you might choose to invest in more fixed-income investments.

The key to investing is to determine your tolerance for risk and be guided by it. If you are going to panic every time the stock market goes down, investing in stocks may not be best for you. Investing in bonds may be the best way for you to grow your wealth.

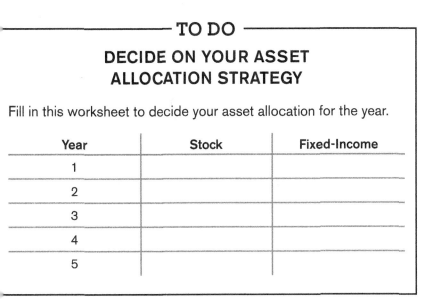

── TO DO ──

DECIDE ON YOUR ASSET ALLOCATION STRATEGY

Fill in this worksheet to decide your asset allocation for the year.

Year	Stock	Fixed-Income
1		
2		
3		
4		
5		

Select Specific Investments

After deciding your asset allocation, the next thing to think about is where to make your investments. This is called diversification; the idea is that you don't want to put all of your eggs in one basket, or all your money in one stock. There are different sub-assets to consider for stocks (such as large companies or small companies) and bonds (such as government bonds or corporate bonds and short-term or longer-term). If you prefer, investment vehicles like mutual funds and ETFs make diversification easier than buying many individual stocks and bonds.

Manage Your Investments

Regularly check your portfolio's performance. If your asset allocation changes drastically, because one category ends up with much more money than the other, you could consider rebalancing it by selling and buying as needed.

Your investments will generate different-sized returns throughout the year, so the simplest strategy for rebalancing your portfolio is to look at all of your assets and tweak them according to your target allocation and market performance. For example, if the stock market has increased more than bonds, you could sell some of your individual stocks or stock ETFs or mutual funds to reinvest that money in your individual bonds or bond ETFs or mutual funds.

CONTRIBUTE TO YOUR 401(k)

It might seem crazy to plan for your golden years before you're even five years out of college, but a 401(k) makes it worth your while to start saving as soon as possible. A 401(k) is an employer-sponsored retirement savings plan that allows you to automatically invest part of your income toward retirement without having to pay income taxes on it until you withdraw the money at a later time.

To set up a 401(k), tell your employer what percentage of your salary you want to put toward it, and that amount will be taken from your paychecks and deposited into your investment account. There are limits to how much you can contribute to your 401(k) each year, but it changes every year. Don't worry about trying to max it out each year; the limits are usually high, and most people don't max out for the year. You can contribute the amount that works best for the budget you created in Chapter 7.

The money in your 401(k) is invested in stock and bond funds, and you can choose how your 401(k) is invested. Different employers will offer different investment options. One of the most common and easiest options is to invest in a *target-date fund*. You might see the target-date fund listed as a 2060 fund or a 2070 fund—that number is the approximate date that you plan to retire and start withdrawing the money.

If you're self-employed and don't have any full-time employees, you can set up a Solo 401(k) and make pretax contributions. If you do have full-time employees, meet with a financial advisor to discuss setting up a 401(k) or other savings plan for your company.

The asset allocation for the fund is based on how long you have until you plan to retire and follows the general principle that younger people can make riskier investments and have a higher proportion of stocks compared to fixed-income investments. Two benefits of a target-date fund are that it is diversified and the asset allocation changes automatically, so you don't have to rebalance your portfolio. If you don't want to participate in a target-date fund, you can choose from a list of mutual funds and ETFs.

Make the Most of Matching

Some companies will match your 401(k) contributions up to a set percentage of your salary or a dollar amount, which means the more you contribute, the more *they* contribute. If you contribute 6 percent of your salary, your company will too, doubling how much goes in. Companies set a limit on the percentage amount they'll match.

The company's contributions will often have something called a vesting date. That means that the money they contribute isn't officially yours until that date. If you're no longer working for the company when that date comes around, all or a percentage of the money goes back to the company. If you're thinking about making a move to a new job, it might be worth it to stick around a little bit longer to hit your vesting date. Check your employer manual or ask someone from human resources to make sure you know when that is.

If you quit your job, you get to keep your 401(k), since it's your money. You'll "roll it over" to the account set up by your new employer, or turn it into an IRA.

START AN INDIVIDUAL RETIREMENT ACCOUNT (IRA)

A 401(k) isn't the only way to save for retirement. Another option is to set up your own individual retirement account (IRA). In fact, it's often a good idea to contribute to your 401(k) *and* an IRA if you can. Once you've hit the percentage limit for how much your company will match on your 401(k), it may make sense to put any additional money you planned to save into an IRA. If you work for a company that doesn't have a 401(k) as part of the benefits package, you'll need to set up your own IRA to start saving for retirement. Some financial planners think that you might not be able to save enough money in a 401(k), so it is helpful to supplement it by also investing in an IRA.

Like with a 401(k), you can choose your asset allocation. The main benefit of an IRA is that your money grows tax-free. The income you earn from interest, dividends, and capital gains compounds each year *and* you don't need to pay taxes on it.

Traditional versus Roth IRAs

There are two main types of IRAs, a traditional IRA and a Roth IRA. The primary difference between them is when you pay income taxes:

- With a **traditional IRA**, your contributions may be tax-deductible in the year you contribute, but you have to pay taxes when you withdraw the money.
- With a **Roth IRA**, your contributions may be not tax-deductible, but you don't have to pay taxes when you withdraw the money if certain conditions are met.

Since you are young, it might make more sense to use a Roth IRA instead of a traditional IRA because you are probably in a lower tax bracket now than you will be when you are ready to retire. You can speak to a financial planner to learn the more nuanced differences between the two, but that is the main one to know.

If you're unsure of what kind of investment plan you should use, go to an IRA provider like Fidelity, Betterment, or Vanguard. They have algorithms, fund options, and financial advisors who can help you choose a plan that works best for your goals.

CONSIDER HIRING A FINANCIAL PLANNER

A financial planner can help you plan for big financial goals, like buying a home, getting out of debt, and saving for retirement.

Choosing a financial planner is a big decision. Before hiring anyone, do your research and make sure they're the right person to help you. Look for Certified Financial Planners (CFP), who are licensed professionals that need to pass a test, continue to take courses, and agree to a code of ethics and standards. Check if they are a *fiduciary*. That means they have to do what is best for you, not what's in their own best interest.

You don't need a financial planner, but there might be times when it's helpful to meet with one to plan for big life changes and your goals. They'll help you get your finances in order.

You Are Combining Finances with Your Partner

It can be helpful to have someone walk you through the process of sharing your finances. It can be a confusing process, and there are different ways to go about it. You might decide to have a joint account and still maintain your personal accounts or to keep your finances completely together or completely separate. It's ultimately up to you and your partner, but it helps to have someone there who knows all the possibilities and who can help you set up plans and goals together.

You Have a Lot of Debt

A financial planner can help you create a strategy for paying off your debt. She can help you set your budget and make decisions such as whether it makes sense to repay all of your debt before you start investing. Decisions like consolidating and refinancing your loans are easier to make when you have a financial planner to advise you.

You Have a Big Windfall

If you suddenly come into a lot of money all at once, it can be difficult to know what to do with it all. A financial planner and a good accountant can help you make a plan for how best to manage your newfound money, as well as make sure you are paying your taxes correctly.

You Are an Entrepreneur

Your finances are more complicated when you own a business. A financial planner can give you suggestions for separating your personal finances from your business finances, finding a system for tracking your business earnings and expenses, and making a plan for paying any employees you may have.

You Want to Buy a House

There are many things to consider when you are buying a home. You need to think about down payments, mortgage options, and more. It will help to have as high of a credit score as possible when applying for a mortgage, and a financial planner can give you advice for raising your credit score and getting your assets together to buy your home.

You Want to Start a Family

A financial planner can help you with budgeting for a baby, such as paying for childcare, medical expenses, and essentials. This might be a good time to think about estate planning, buying life insurance, and saving for college.

You Want to Plan for Retirement

A financial planner can help you customize your retirement plan. If you meet with a financial planner who is also a portfolio manager, she can help you create a portfolio that meets your goals. You can tell her your expected retirement date, your risk tolerance, and your current and projected future income, and she can help you make a plan that works for you.

Points to Remember

 The earlier you start investing, the better, thanks to compounding interest.

 There are many ways to invest, including individual stocks and bonds, mutual funds, and ETFs. Each has a different risk and level of involvement.

 Although you're probably a long way from retirement, setting up a 401(k) or IRA account now will pay off in the long run.

 Working with a financial planner can make navigating tricky financial situations easier.

Chapter 9
Figure Out Your Living Space

You've left the dorm—or an off-campus house or apartment—and now it's time to find somewhere new to call home. You can find a place by yourself and live alone, you can live with a roommate, or you can save some money and move back home with your parents. There are pros and cons to each, but the most important thing is to find the place that works for you.

It takes time and energy to find somewhere new to live, but when everything comes together and you're all moved into your new place, it feels wonderful. These tips will simplify the process of finding a rental and furnishing it, and eventually buying a house.

LIVING WITH YOUR PARENTS

You might decide to save up money by moving back in with your parents for a few months or years after you graduate. Moving there now doesn't mean you have to stay forever, and it can be a good option for saving enough money to rent or buy a nice place when you can afford it. If you do move home, talk about expectations in advance, including whether you'll pay any rent or what you'll do to pitch in around the house. Living at home can help you pay off any student loans and debt sooner so you can start saving and hit your financial goals.

FIND A HOUSE OR APARTMENT

It's time to start looking at listings online, visiting apartments and houses to rent, and finding your home. Find somewhere you're comfortable, without too long of a commute to work, in a neighborhood you like, that is within your price range. It doesn't have to be a place you live forever, but it does have to be somewhere you can see yourself living for a few years and can afford. Think of renting as a stepping-stone to buying a home. You have somewhere to live while you save up to buy the right home when you are ready.

Know What You Can Afford

Before you can start searching, you need to have an idea of your price range. One general guideline for renting is to spend no more than 30 percent of your monthly income (before taxes) on rent. That's easier said than done in expensive cities like New York City and San Francisco. Whether or not you adhere to the 30 percent guideline, you may find it helpful when determining what you can afford. Look at your budget and think about your other monthly expenses and your financial goals, like paying off your student loans and credit card debt.

When you are budgeting, think about any extra costs you might need to pay such as an application fee, security and pet deposits, and a broker's fee.

Consider a Roommate

Find someone you're comfortable living with for a while, because most leases run for at least a year. You might absolutely love someone...but not love living with them. If you're lucky, you might have friends in the area that you could live with. If not, you might be able to find someone through a friend of a friend, your alumni network, or an app like Roomi, SpareRoom USA, Cirtru, or Circle.

When you narrow down your potential roommates, have an honest conversation about your preferences, how you'll split expenses, and how you'll divide up cleaning, chores, and basic necessities. Discuss "house rules," such as how you feel about overnight guests, how clean you'll keep common rooms, and any potential pet peeves (like having significant others basically move in, hosting parties, or borrowing each other's things).

Find the Perfect Place

You and your roommates can find a house or apartment on your own by looking at listings on rental websites like *Zillow*, *StreetEasy*, or *Trulia*. This gives you the freedom to find exactly what you need in an apartment (and what you want too) and lets you find a place within your price range. However, apartment hunting this way can be a bit more time-consuming, so it might make sense to hire someone to help you.

If you feel like you need help narrowing your search, hire a broker who can help you find places that match your wants and needs. Brokers know the neighborhoods where you're looking and might have an inside scoop on listings before they hit the market. They might even help you negotiate your lease and monthly rent.

The downside of a broker is they cost money in the form of the aptly named broker's fee. The fee varies depending on the broker.

If you've found a place you like, either online or through a broker, check it out before committing to a lease. You might find that the rooms look bright and spacious online, but that the photos were taken at a favorable angle or that the photos were edited. If you are moving into an apartment, see the condition of the building itself and get a feel for the neighborhood.

Visit the neighborhood in the morning and at night so you know what it's like at different times of the day; walk around and go to restaurants and coffee shops to get a feel for what it will be like to live in the area.

Negotiating Your Rent

If you've found a place you'd like to live in, the next step is to negotiate your rent. If a broker helped you find the place, she can help you with the negotiations, but you can do it yourself as well. You could offer to extend your lease term to two years in exchange for lower rent. It can be a hassle for a landlord to find new tenants, so this is a win-win for both of you. You can negotiate for other lease provisions, such as having the apartment or house painted or requiring the landlord to make necessary repairs before your move-in date.

If the answer is no, try again when your lease is about to expire. By then you will have proven to be a star tenant, and you may have earned a little goodwill from your landlord that you can use in negotiations.

Talk to your landlord to see how exactly they want the rent paid. Can each roommate pay their share separately? Can you pay electronically somehow, or do they need a check?

Prepare Your Paperwork

When you apply for the apartment you want, you and any roommates will need to fill out paperwork. The exact forms might vary from state to state, but in general you'll need a recent pay stub, a photo ID, and an application. If you are self-employed, you might be asked to show more federal income tax returns and bank statements. The requirements depend on what your soon-to-be landlord asks for, so reach out to her before you put in the application so you have everything ready to go.

Agreeing to a Lease

If you are approved to rent an apartment or house, the next step is reading your lease. It will usually stipulate the length of your lease, the annual rent, and the amount of your security deposit. It should specify details like whether your landlord is responsible for maintenance, if pets are allowed, if you can add decorative touches like wallpaper or different paint colors, if you are responsible for paying for any utilities, and what happens if you want to move out before the lease is up.

Depending on your income, a landlord may require that you have a guarantor or cosigner. Some landlords require your income to be at least forty times the monthly rent. If you don't meet that threshold, they may require you to have a guarantor or cosigner on your lease. Besides turning to your wealthy great aunt, there are services like Insurent or TheGuarantors that will serve as your guarantor or cosigner, for a fee.

BUY FURNITURE AND ESSENTIALS

Now that you have an apartment, you need to furnish it. If you have a roommate or multiple roommates, you can split up the list. Furniture and decor can be expensive, but you can usually find some good deals if you shop around. You can always upgrade when you have more money.

─── TO DO ───
LIST YOUR APARTMENT ESSENTIALS

Remember when you went off to college and had a college packing checklist? Here's one for your adult apartment. You may already have some of these items, so fill in any gaps you're missing. Use the blank spots to add other items you might need.

Kitchen
- Kitchen table and chairs
- Measuring spoons and measuring cup
- Saucepan
- Skillet
- Stockpot
- Baking sheets
- Mixing bowls
- Spatula
- Slotted spoon
- Whisk
- Wooden stirring spoon
- Cutting board
- Utensils

- Set of dishes, glasses, and mugs
- Chef's knife
- Paring knife
- Bread knife
- Kitchen scissors
- Oven mitts
- Dish towels
- Trash can
- Food storage containers
- Colander
- _____
- _____

Bathroom

- Toothbrush holder
- Small trash can
- Shower curtain and liner
- Bath mat
- Bath towels
- Hand towels
- Washcloths
- Plunger
- Toilet brush set

- _____

- _____

Bedroom

- Bed
- Dresser
- Nightstand
- Two sets of sheets
- Pillows
- Blanket
- Closet hangers
- Curtains
- Nightstand lamp

- _____

- _____

Living Room

- Couch
- Coffee table
- Armchairs
- Curtains
- Television
- Television stand

- _____

- _____

Other

- Carbon monoxide detector
- Smoke detector
- Step stool
- Cleaning supplies like dish soap, all-purpose cleaners, laundry detergent, toilet bowl cleaner, and bathroom cleaner
- Hammer
- Screwdriver, both flat-head and Phillips-head
- Extension cords
- Vacuum cleaner
- Mop
- Broom

- _____

- _____

PLAN IF YOU WANT TO BUY A HOME

You might not be ready to buy your first home yet, but there are things you can start doing now so you're ready when that day comes. It might seem a long way off, especially when you're still figuring out how to decorate your new apartment, but the sooner you start saving, the quicker you can buy a place of your own.

Brainstorm Your Dream Home and Location

This is the fun part! Start thinking about your dream home and neighborhood. If you are buying a home with a partner, come up with a list of your negotiables and nonnegotiables together. Write down things you need and want, including the number of bedrooms you'd like, how long the commute would be, whether you want a newer home or an older one, the quality of the school district, and how much you'd be willing to spend on renovations.

Once you have your list in place, take a look at some listings to see the price range of your dream house. Is it within your budget to start saving for a house at that price? Perfect! Time to get started on saving for a down payment. If not, look at your wants again and see what you're flexible on. Maybe you can get by with only two bedrooms instead of three or go without a finished basement. Once you've found a price range that fit your needs and your most important wants, you can begin to budget for buying your home.

Start Saving Money

Once you get closer to actually buying a house, a number of costs like a down payment, mortgage, and real estate taxes will be required. It's a big and important purchase, and it will be helpful to have a team of experts (a real estate agent, bank employee or mortgage lender, and lawyer) walk you through all the steps of buying your home. In the meantime, work on paying off any debt and improving your credit score so you can qualify for a mortgage.

When you've saved up all your money and you're finally ready to buy your home, it's time to find a real estate agent and start visiting houses. But for now, it's best to just start saving your money until you're ready to get to the next steps.

Points to Remember

 If you decide to move back home to save money, discuss the arrangement with your parents to be sure everyone is on the same page with how it will work.

 Before you start looking for apartments to rent, use the budgeting tips in Chapter 7 to see how much you can afford to pay. Find a roommate if necessary.

 Remember that the rent listed and points noted in the lease are negotiable.

 Educate yourself about home buying so if you choose to go that route in the future, you are prepared for the process.

Part 3

WELLNESS

There is nothing more important than your physical and mental health. You can't control your health 100 percent, but there are actions you can take to live a healthier lifestyle so you can control what you can and manage what you can't.

The first few years after college, and particularly the first, can be physically and emotionally draining. You have long workdays and less control over your schedule and more responsibilities in your personal and professional life. Maybe you are searching for a job, and your self-confidence plummets every time you get a rejection email. Maybe your five-year plan included goals about cooking healthy meals for yourself, but you have no idea where to start. Maybe you feel like you're the only one who doesn't have your life together.

It's a tough transition, but you will get through it. Right now, the most important thing is to take good care of yourself, and this section will help you learn important self-care skills that you'll use your entire life.

Chapter 10

Take Care of Your Physical Health

When you don't feel well, it has a ripple effect on everything in your life, from your mental health to your concentration and productivity. This chapter has easy-to-follow tips for finding a fitness routine that you enjoy, eating well, and creating an evening routine you look forward to that helps you unwind from the day.

CREATE AND STICK TO A FITNESS ROUTINE

There are countless reasons why working out is good for your mental and physical health. A regular fitness routine can:

- Boost your energy.
- Make you happier.
- Decrease stress.
- Support your immune system.
- Combat some diseases and health conditions.

- Improve your sleep.
- Strengthen your muscles.
- Increase productivity.
- Help you maintain a healthy weight.
- Enhance your sex life.

Make working out part of your weekly routine. Whether you already run marathons or consider running errands to be your cardio, you can cultivate a fitness routine that makes working out work for you.

Choose Three

Try different classes and apps to find at least three workouts you enjoy. Having a variety helps make sure you balance cardio and strength training, plus it keeps you from getting bored. Programs and apps like ClassPass, FitReserve, Daily Burn, and Nike Training Club—or gyms with class offerings—make it fun and easy to experiment and find what you like.

Create Consistency

Schedule your workouts the same way you do your meetings, deadlines, and social life. At the beginning of each week, choose the days you want to exercise and the type of workout you want to complete (such as yoga, a three-mile run, or "ab day") so you plan for it in your day. Planning ahead will help you stay accountable.

Consider using an app to take some of the guesswork out of planning your fitness routine. Some workout apps will create your workout schedule and include variations that make sure you don't forget your arms, abs, legs, or cardio. Check out SWEAT, Tone It Up, Aaptiv, or Daily Burn, for example. Apps like Runkeeper, Map-MyRun, or Nike Run Club can help you create a custom running training plan based on your starting point and goals. You could use fitness trackers like one from Fitbit or Garmin to make sure you're reaching other goals like walking 10,000 steps a day.

It can be helpful to have an accountability group: Find yoga, Spinning, or running buddies and encourage one another to reach a shared goal.

TO DO

COMPLETE ONE MAJOR FITNESS GOAL

Take the fitness goals from your five-year plan and start working on them one at a time. Having goals helps you stay committed, even when it is raining or snowing and you'd much rather be curled up on the couch than going to the gym. You will feel proud, happy, and excited about your accomplishments, and those feelings and endorphins will make you want to continue to work out and train for your next big goal.

Break It Down
Break your big goals into smaller, more manageable ones. If you want to do a three-minute plank, start with thirty seconds then gradually increase the time until three minutes doesn't seem like forever. If you've never run a mile, don't make it your goal to run a marathon by the end of the month. Instead, run thirty minutes a few days a week, then build up to a 5K, a 10K, a half-marathon, and finally a full marathon (if you're up for it)!

Celebrate Your Accomplishments
One of the benefits of breaking a big goal into smaller ones is that you have more opportunities to celebrate what you've achieved along the way. You might not always get a medal like you do if you finish a race, but take a minute to appreciate your hard work and how far you've come before pushing for the next literal or metaphorical sprint.

FOCUS ON NUTRITION

You no longer have access to the dining hall, with its multiple healthy (a fully stocked salad bar) and not-so-healthy (that frozen yogurt station) options. Now you're the one doing the grocery shopping and cooking, so you can make healthier choices.

Healthy eating can boost your heart health, prevent diabetes, improve your mental health, reduce your risk of cancer, and help you maintain a healthy weight. A balanced diet will sharpen your focus, raise energy levels, and improve digestion. People have different approaches to healthy eating, but remembering some basic facts and guidelines can help you feel good, whether you prefer your diet to be vegetarian, vegan, gluten-free, dairy-free, pescatarian, or to include everything in moderation.

You eat a balanced diet when you get all, or most, of the various food groups in appropriate amounts. (The food pyramid guide to servings has been replaced by the US Department of Agriculture's MyPlate, which shows portions each food group should have on your plate at every meal: www.choosemyplate.gov.)

Eat Nutrient-Dense Foods

Nutrient-dense foods are high in vitamins, minerals, and other healthy nutrients. They have little or no added fats, added sugars, added salt, or other high-sodium ingredients. Try keeping these foods in your cabinets and fridge so you can always put together a healthy meal: vegetables, fruit, whole grains, seafood, eggs, beans and peas, unsalted nuts and seeds, dairy, and lean meats and poultry.

Keep It "Clean"

Clean eating is having a marketing moment, but it's been around forever. People weren't hunting and gathering at Trader Joe's or eating packaged foods during the medieval era—they were eating foods that could be found in their natural state.

When you "eat clean," you eat whole foods and skip processed foods with additives, preservatives, chemicals, dyes, trans fats, high-fructose corn syrup, and anything you can't pronounce, according to the healthy living publication *EatingWell*. Avoid refined grains (like white rice and white bread, which are processed), unhealthy fats, and foods with lots of added sugar and salt.

Let Them Eat Cake...Sometimes

Many restrictive diets cut out entire food groups, such as gluten, dairy, soy, refined sugar, and coffee. It can be difficult to stay on such a restrictive diet, especially when you enjoy going out to eat with friends and family and don't want to interrogate the server each time you order. (Of course, if you have a severe food allergy, you must ask a list of questions and confirm that the kitchen is aware of the severity of your dietary needs.)

If you find that when you're on a limited diet, all you want is everything you are "not allowed" to enjoy, you may want to try the 80/20 approach. That's when you stick to the diet 80 percent of the time, allowing yourself to eat what you want 20 percent of the time (you can adjust the proportions to 90/10 if you want to be a little stricter). It's easier to maintain healthy eating for the long-term when you're giving yourself some leeway.

Cook Your Own Food

When you make your own meals, you know all the ingredients and measurements. When you go out to eat or order takeout, the portion sizes are usually oversized, you're not certain of the ingredients being used, and it's expensive. Look at your calendar at the start of the week to plan your meals. Find recipes you want to make for each meal, after checking to see what you have in your fridge and pantry already, and make a grocery shopping list so you don't forget anything.

Try Meal Prepping

When you've had a busy day at work, it can be tempting to order takeout, go out to eat, or have a bowl of cereal for dinner because you don't feel like cooking and cleaning up. To avoid that temptation, try meal prepping, which is when you cook all (or some) of your meals for the week at once. There are two main meal-prepping strategies:

1. One is to make all your meals for the week once a week. Pack servings in individual containers and either refrigerate or freeze.

2. The other option is to prepare a basic meal foundation—roasted veggies, quinoa, and grilled chicken, for example—and then during the week you can switch up the toppings like hummus, sun-dried tomatoes, feta or cheddar cheese, black beans, or guacamole to make customized grain bowls or salads.

Even though the day you meal prep might be busy, you'll save time during the week, and you'll save money because going out to eat or ordering in gets expensive.

DRINK RESPONSIBLY

Your beer pong and flip cup days in crowded fraternity houses might be over, but you might still drink socially after college. You might have a drink or two at happy hour, on a date, when you are out to dinner with friends, or when you are curled up on the couch with your roommate catching up on your favorite TV show. You've probably heard this a thousand times before, but the most important thing is to drink responsibly if you choose to drink at all. Know your limit, never drink and drive, space out your drinks, and drink plenty of water throughout the night. Be aware of signs that you could have an alcohol problem like binge drinking, having negative repercussions on your personal or professional life, or feeling like you are physically and psychologically dependent on drinking.

Vaping is becoming increasingly popular because some people view it as less dangerous than smoking. It *is* dangerous, however, and doctors say that it has been linked to lung injury, heart disease, and death.

If you think you might have a problem with alcohol or drugs, talk to your doctor and find a treatment plan.

GET ENOUGH SLEEP

To function at your best during the day, you need to get enough sleep at night. Adults should get quality, uninterrupted sleep for seven to eight hours a night. Getting the recommended amount of sleep can improve your immune system, reduce stress, boost your mood, decrease your risk of serious health problems like diabetes and heart disease, and help you think clearly and perform your best at work. Keep all these health benefits in mind and turn off the light and your phone instead of scrolling on *Instagram*, checking posts on *Facebook*, or binge-watching Netflix.

Create an Evening Routine

A good evening routine can help you transition from the hustle and bustle of the day to the tranquility of bedtime. Find what works for you, like taking a warm bath or shower, drinking a hot cup of decaf tea, reading a book, journaling, listening to quiet music, or doing an elaborate skincare routine. Start your "wind-down time" an hour or two before your bedtime.

When you get home from work, you could cook a healthy dinner or have something you've meal prepped, then get cozy on the couch and watch TV or a movie. It can be relaxing to watch TV and think about the characters and plotlines of your favorite shows, as opposed to dwelling on work and worries. Enjoy your TV time, but turn it off and try to stop looking at other electronic devices an hour or two before bedtime.

Be Careful with Blue Lights

Electronics emit rays called "blue light"; blue light makes you feel more awake. Blue light has a short wavelength that makes more of an impact on your melatonin levels than other types of light, according to the National Sleep Foundation. Melatonin is a natural hormone that helps control your circadian rhythm. You feel sleepy when your melatonin levels are higher and more awake when they are lower. The pineal gland in your brain starts to release melatonin a few hours before a normal bedtime.

Using blue light–emitting devices (such as TVs, laptops, smartphones, and fluorescent lights) before bed delays your ability to fall asleep and may decrease your REM sleep, which is the time you are getting the deep, high-quality sleep your body needs. (If you prefer to read on a tablet or e-reader, you should be able to adjust the blue light settings or download an app to make that possible.)

Make Your Bedroom a Calming Place

Think of your bedroom as a cozy oasis. You'll have an easier time falling asleep if your bedroom is dark, quiet, and a comfortable temperature. Try these tips:

- If your bedroom is bright even when you close the blinds or curtains, give blackout curtains or a sleep mask a try.
- If your bedroom is noisy at night, try a sound machine to block out unwanted noises.
- An air conditioner, heater, or an extra blanket can help you get the temperature just right.
- Use a bedside lamp with a light dimmer or a low-watt light bulb so the bright lights don't make it harder to fall asleep.

Set a Bedtime

Going to sleep and waking up at the same time every day will help set your circadian rhythm, which is that twenty-four-hour internal clock that makes you sleepy when it's nighttime and energized and awake when it's daytime, according to the National Sleep Foundation. A bedtime routine can also improve your sleep quality.

Take the time you have to wake up in the morning and work backward seven or eight hours to find out the time that you should be curled up in bed with the lights out. If you're an expert procrastinator, set an alarm to remind you when it's time to start getting ready for bed or turn off the lights.

When You Just Can't Seem to Fall Asleep

It's frustrating to be in bed and unable to fall asleep. There are several common reasons:

- Your daytime habits could be contributing to your difficulty falling asleep or staying asleep. Try to schedule energy-boosting activities, like coffee dates and workouts, earlier in the day.
- What you eat, and when, can affect your sleep. Avoid eating heavy meals and foods or drinks with a lot of refined sugar or caffeine a few hours before bedtime.
- Anxiety can make it difficult to fall asleep. Have you ever been lying in bed thinking about your to-do list for the next day or things that are making you worried or sad? Before you try to sleep, write out tomorrow's to-do list or journal.

Sometimes just writing about what's on your mind can help you "turn off" that constant chatter in your head so you can fall asleep.

If you frequently feel anxious or depressed or find yourself unable to sleep and it is affecting your physical and mental health, speak to your physician, psychologist, or psychiatrist to address the issue.

Points to Remember

- Finding a variety of ways to exercise can help you stay fit. Set goals and celebrate milestones to keep yourself motivated.

- Cook healthy meals at home—it's the best way to know that you are eating nutrient-dense foods that are low in additives and preservatives.

- Getting enough sleep is a crucial element in your overall health. Wind down in a way that works for you, shut off your screens, and try to maintain the same bedtime every day.

Chapter 11

Take Care of Your Mental Health

Your mental health is just as important as your physical health, yet there is still a societal stigma that can make it difficult to talk about or address. You might not know when and how to seek help if you are struggling. This stigma can make people feel ashamed or guilty about reporting how they feel. But think about it: Would you think twice about calling a doctor if you got strep or broke your arm?

Self-care and "me time" are big buzzwords right now. It may seem like the combination of a bubble bath, tea, and a face mask can magically make everything better. But self-care is really about taking care of yourself by exercising, sleeping, and eating well—and taking care of your mental health. In this chapter, you'll learn strategies for boosting your mental health, such as taking breaks, asking for help when you need it, saying no to plans without feeling guilty, finding hobbies, boosting your resilience, decreasing negative self-talk and rumination, cultivating mindfulness, and limiting social comparison. It will help you feel comfortable treating your mental health just as seriously as your physical health by learning how to find and choose a therapist and type of therapy.

FOCUS ON WORK-LIFE INTEGRATION

Work-life balance is a myth. There is never going to be a perfect equilibrium between your personal life and professional life. There are going to be times you need to focus more on work and times you need to focus more on your personal life, and your priorities may shift day to day. *Work-life integration* is a more realistic description, because it allows for flexibility and doesn't require a perfect (and unattainable) balance.

Set Boundaries at Work

Every job is different, and some will always require longer hours than others, plus require employees to adjust their schedules during "busy" seasons or "busy" times. No matter where you work, you can set some boundaries to avoid burnout. Talk to your boss or someone who has been on your team longer than you to find out the expectations for your work hours and how accessible you need to be when you are not in the office.

Set Expectations

While it may be easy to check emails while on a Spin bike, respond to work emails when you're watching a movie, or spend a few hours working on the weekend from the comfort of your bed, find out what is expected. That way, you're clear on which client or work-related emails and calls you need to answer right away and what can wait until you get back to the office. There's no harm in quickly scanning your email after hours and on weekends to check if there is anything that absolutely has to be done, but use your judgment as to what's immediately pressing and what can wait so you don't feel like you are constantly on call...unless you actually are. If you aren't sure whether something is urgent, ask. You could say something like "I can work on that. Is this something you need tonight or can I get it to you by noon tomorrow?" That way you'll show that you saw the email and provided a plan for when you could complete it. If you know it isn't urgent but you want to show that you've received it, you can say "I'll work on that first thing to-morrow morning. Have a good evening!" (You could also wait until the next day to respond, which is why it's helpful to know whether your boss *actually* expects email responses right away or if it's just that she always tackles her inbox at 9 p.m.)

Let's say you get an assignment during "normal business hours," but you have a long to-do list and you aren't sure what needs to be prioritized. You could tell your boss something such as "I am happy to work on that assignment. Right now I am working on X, Y, and Z. I want to make sure I get you everything you need. What prioritization works best for you?"

Truly Be "Off the Clock"

Once you are able to set boundaries at work, be sure you are using your time out of work for yourself. Maybe you'll go for a three-mile run every morning, visit the farmer's market, make dinner plans with friends, or binge-watch a show until Netflix wonders if you are still watching. Doing things you enjoy will help keep your mind off work. Whatever it is, give yourself time to relax and unwind.

Speaking of being "off the clock," take your vacation days. Set boundaries and an out-of-office autoreply for your vacations. Your autoreply can provide contact info for a coworker who has been designated to handle matters that cannot wait and will call you if anything urgent comes up. If you are uncomfortable totally discon- necting, scan for important emails once in the morning and once in the evening and delegate any immediate action items to coworkers back in the office.

ASK FOR HELP

There will be times when you need help—whether it's with a per- sonal problem or an overwhelming work project. It would be great if people would notice and automatically offer their help, but even the most supportive friends, family members, partners, and coworkers can't read your mind. Sometimes they don't notice that you have been sending signals that you are stressed, sad, or overwhelmed.

Ask for help when you need it, whether you'd like a family mem- ber to join you for an important doctor appointment that you're nervous about, a friend to talk to after a terrible day at work, or a coworker to help you when you're struggling with an important pro- ject. You could say something like "I have an important doctor's appointment this week, and it would mean a lot to me if you could be there to support me. Would you be able to come on Thursday at noon?" At work try saying something like "Would you mind re- viewing the proposal before I send it to the client? Your feedback always makes the proposals stronger." Your friends, family, partner, and coworkers care about you and want to help, but they don't al- ways know what you need, so you have to ask.

SCHEDULE REST AND RELAXATION TIME

Do you ever feel guilty taking breaks because you hear a nagging voice reminding you just how much you could or should be doing? If that sounds familiar, add "time off" to your to-do list to prevent burnout and ensure time to recharge so you are more productive when you are working.

If you find yourself wondering how the heck people manage to set aside an hour (or even fifteen minutes) to do nothing, look at your calendar and add it in. Just like you schedule your meetings at work, your social life, and your workouts, schedule your R&R too. You'll be more likely to remember to take time to relax if it's a scheduled event in your calendar. These ideas can help you integrate this mind-set into your daily life so it feels more natural to do nothing.

Ban "Busy"

When someone asks you how you are doing, how often do you say "I'm so busy!" or "Things are so jam-packed right now…"? Even if you don't find yourself talking about how busy you are, you have probably heard your friends, coworkers, and family talk about just how overwhelmed they are at work. Be mindful of how often you tell other people how busy you are, and instead talk about your feelings, what's new with you, and what is exciting you. While you're it, work on actually being less busy by saying no sometimes.

Skip "Should" and Say No

When you find yourself saying that you "should" do something, ask yourself if you really want to or if you are only doing it because you think it's expected of you. Sometimes you have to do things that you really don't want to do but must, like a project at work that is boring but has to be done or going to the doctor for your annual physical. But there will be other tasks, events, or appointments that are optional, and you can give yourself the gift of opting out of those.

Be honest and say no to proposed plans you truly don't want to take part in. Instead of going to happy hour, it's okay to watch a few episodes of your favorite TV show, take your dog for a long walk in the park, read a book, take a hot bath, meditate, go to a yoga class, or do what you really want to do.

That being said, it's rude to agree to and then cancel plans last minute, so try not to do that either. Sometimes you really do have to cancel plans because you have to work late or don't feel well, but when you already know you don't want to do something, just say no in advance.

When you have things on the calendar that you *want* to do, reframe how you talk or think about them. Something as simple as shifting from "I have to" to "I want to," "I'm excited to," or "I get to" can reframe it as something you are looking forward to and want, instead of an obligation or imposition.

You can say no sometimes and still be a supportive friend, family member, coworker, and partner. Recognize which events are important and show you prioritize the relationship by going to a friend's birthday dinner, showing up at your coworker's improv show, or planning the best Galentine's Day ever for a friend who is going through a breakup. Know that there are times when it's okay to say "Sorry, can't make it this time."

Saying no can take some practice if you're not used to it. Thank the person for the invitation, but respond that you won't be able to make it. You can offer an honest reason if you choose, but you don't have to explain yourself. Show that you care about them by making plans for another time.

RENEW OR CREATE A NEW HOBBY

Hobbies help you enjoy yourself and constantly learn and improve. In some instances, a hobby like photography, blogging, or writing a novel can become your new full-time job or something you do to earn extra income. (Don't put too much pressure on yourself, though; the real goal is to find an activity that makes you happy.)

Try New Things

Is there anything you've always wanted to learn or something that looks like it might be fun, like a foreign language, watercolor painting, or woodworking? Try it! (If you aren't sure what you want to do, think about what you enjoyed when you were younger.) Learning new skills builds brain power.

You can dive into some hobbies without instruction, but there are some that will be more fun if you take classes or go to meetups where you can learn new skills *and* find like-minded new friends. Group classes are especially helpful if you are moving to a city where you don't already have an established friend group.

Make Time for It

Once you've found a hobby you enjoy, make time for it! When you say no to things you don't want to do and set boundaries at work, you'll find that you will have more time to prioritize your hobbies.

It's Okay to Quit Hobbies

The purpose of hobbies is to have fun. If you try something and realize you don't enjoy it, it's okay to quit. Give something else a try, then another thing, and another thing until you have a handful (or more!) of hobbies that make you happy.

DEVELOP HEALTHY COPING MECHANISMS

When you are feeling anxious, sad, or burned out, it is essential to know coping mechanisms that make you feel better. Amy Morin, a licensed clinical social worker, wrote about coping strategies for the health website *Verywell Health*. According to Morin, it's important to have both problem-based coping mechanisms and emotion-based coping mechanisms.

Problem-Based Coping Mechanisms

Problem-based coping mechanisms are helpful when there is a problem you can solve by changing your situation. If you are stressed at work, for example, you could speak to your boss about ways to decrease your workload or ideas for dealing with a difficult coworker who takes credit for your ideas, interrupts you in meetings, or is just hard to get along with.

Here are some hands-on ways to problem-solve:

- Create a to-do list if you are feeling disorganized.
- Have an honest conversation when you are upset about something.
- Accept help when it's offered.
- Ask for help when you need it.
- Talk to a coworker or a mental health professional.

Use problem-solving ideas to fix the situation, and if they don't work, it might be time to remove the stressor from your life. If you are miserable at work, for example, start applying for a new job.

Emotion-Based Coping Mechanisms

Morin explains that emotion-based coping is beneficial when you need to look after your emotional health and either can't or don't want to change your situation because you expect that it can get better.

If you are having difficulty in a relationship; fighting with a friend; caring for a loved one who is sick; or feeling sad, lonely, stressed, angry, jealous, or irritable, emotion-based coping mechanisms can help.

Here are some ways to address emotion-based issues:

- Work out
- Read
- Cook
- Listen to music
- Spend time with friends and family or your partner
- Watch television
- Take a bath
- Meditate
- Write in a journal
- Drink tea
- Go for a walk
- Write a list of things that make you grateful
- Practice breathing exercises

If none of these ideas work, talk to a mental health professional about addressing the issue.

Proactive Coping Mechanisms

Proactive coping mechanisms can help you manage future issues before they become overwhelming, according to Morin. If you are sad because your partner got into grad school and you are about to be in a long-distance relationship, schedule phone dates and visits so you have plans to look forward to, for example. Here are some ways to get ahead of problems before they come to a head:

- Pay attention to signs that you are feeling burned out, sad, or stressed as soon as possible so you can start using coping mechanisms, including speaking to a therapist if you need to, before your emotions feel overwhelming. You might notice that you are having a hard time falling and staying asleep, you can't concentrate at work, you don't feel motivated, your heart races, you've become nervous in social situations, or you are stymied by a task at work that is usually a breeze.

- Implement problem-based coping mechanisms and emotion-based coping mechanisms as soon as you start to notice that you aren't feeling well.
- Take good care of yourself. Get enough sleep, eat nutritious foods, drink enough water, surround yourself with a strong support network, exercise, and relax.

Avoid Unhealthy Coping Mechanisms

There are many healthy, productive ways to cope with difficult circumstances. But, as Morin cautions, there are unhealthy ways to try to cope, such as excessive drinking, smoking cigarettes or vaping, or doing drugs; oversleeping; shopping for things you don't actually need or want; and avoiding the issue. Those things may seem tempting in the moment, but they are likely to make the problem worse. At best, they're only short-term "solutions" that fail to address the root causes.

BUILD YOUR RESILIENCE

Being resilient is a key part of living a healthy life. According to the American Psychological Association's definition, resilience is how you adapt to adversity, trauma, stress, and failure. It's how you "bounce back" from difficult experiences. Being resilient doesn't mean that you can change what unfortunate thing happened in the past, like a breakup, getting fired, or fighting with a friend; it means you can control how you react to a lousy situation and what you may be able to learn from it.

Decrease Negative Thinking

Have you ever experienced something upsetting and replayed what happened and what you could have done differently? Or maybe you think about what you don't like about a situation, and rehash the same complaints and criticisms continuously. When you have trouble controlling your negative thoughts and obsessively repeat the same thoughts again and again like a broken record, it's called rumination. This negative thinking can be a symptom of anxiety and depression. When you feel like you can't control your ruminations, you may feel exhausted, overwhelmed, and distracted.

Rumination can keep you from identifying ways to solve the problem or from moving on. Make a list of the problems you are ruminating about and identify actionable ways to problem-solve for each. Some circumstances can't be solved, such as a friend's illness, in which case all you can do is be there for them. Another strategy is to try to take your mind off whatever is making you upset by going for a run, meditating, doing breathing exercises, talking to a friend, or journaling about what is upsetting you, then trying your best to leave it on the page.

── TO DO ──
DECREASE NEGATIVE SELF-TALK

"I'm bad at math," "I'm a slow writer," "I'll never find love." Sound familiar? Negative self-talk is that nagging, critical voice in your head that tells you that you aren't good enough and won't be successful. It diminishes your self-esteem and changes how you perceive and react to events. If you are let go from a job for financial reasons, you may still worry that it's because you made a mistake or weren't good at your job.

continued on next page

Negative self-talk can make you less resilient because to be resilient you need to believe in your ability to overcome adversity. You may become less motivated and start to feel hopeless, rather than optimistic, in control, and hopeful. Affirmations or mantras can help to quiet your negative self-talk.

It can be hard to silence the inner critic, but it's an important skill to practice. Here are some techniques:

- Discuss how you feel with your friends and family so they can help you find and acknowledge your strengths.
- Shift your thinking by reflecting on what you have accomplished in the past, how much you've improved, and the strengths and talents that come to you naturally.
- Distract yourself with positive activities like working out, cooking, watching a movie, enjoying one of your hobbies, or getting together with friends.
- Listen to your negative self-talk, then write down it down in your journal and counter it with opposite phrases like "I am smart and talented," "I am successful," and "I am a confident public speaker."
- Write down your positive affirmations and keep them on a Post-it on your bathroom mirror, write them in your journal at night, or say them to yourself in the morning as you are heading out the door.

When you have positive thoughts about yourself and your life, you will start to believe them, and they can turn into a beneficial self-fulfilling prophecy. The key is to repeat them frequently so they drown out your negative self-talk and rewire your thinking patterns.

Try Not to Jump to the Worst Possible Outcome

You know when someone says "We need to talk," and you immediately jump to the conclusion that you're going to be fired? Expecting the worst outcome, sometimes without any real evidence, is called catastrophizing. When you assume that the worst outcome will happen, it is stressful and scary and harder to be resilient. Question your catastrophic thinking to see if you could unknowingly be blowing things out of proportion. Ask yourself if there is any evidence that the worst will, in fact, happen, and see if there is anything you could do to prevent an unfortunate situation from getting worse or to decrease your worry.

Reframe How You Think about Failure

You have to be resilient when things go wrong, like when you break up with someone, make a big mistake at work, or get in a fight with a friend. You might think that you "failed" at something or that you are a "failure." No one is perfect—maybe you and your partner both could have communicated better and been more supportive, the mistake you made at work was avoidable, or the fight with a friend was partially your fault. Still, try not to jump to the conclusion that because one thing didn't go well, nothing will go well in the future.

To reframe the situation, think about what you learned from it and ask yourself if there is anything you want to do differently in the future. Forgive yourself so you can move forward instead of getting stuck replaying the past.

CULTIVATE MINDFULNESS

Another way to improve your overall mental health is to practice mindfulness. Mindfulness is the concept of living in the present moment and being aware of your thoughts and emotions without being judgmental. Instead of thinking about the past or worrying about the future, you focus on the present. Mindfulness can decrease stress and rumination and may help prevent or decrease symptoms of anxiety and depression.

Don't Push Away the Feelings

Let's say you are sad because three of your friends went out for dinner and they didn't invite you. You feel left out, but it's probably not just about the one dinner. Maybe it has become a pattern with this friend group and you often feel excluded, or you think it is a pattern because you've felt this way about other group friendships. Maybe you react to the one dinner invite so strongly because it reminds you of a time when you felt lonely. Try to understand exactly how you are feeling, and why.

It is hard to experience negative emotions like sadness, anger, jealousy, or guilt. Try to allow yourself to feel the emotion fully so you can process it and understand the causes better. You may be able to learn from your emotions, or recover more quickly, if you feel them instead of distracting yourself or being in denial.

Try Not to Be Self-Critical

When difficult emotions come up, try not to be judgmental or deflect them. If you find yourself thinking "I shouldn't be sad about this," "I don't know why I'm so mad about this," or "I wish I didn't get stressed so easily," try to experience the emotions, even when they are uncomfortable.

Mindfulness in Daily Life

Anything that makes you slow down and be more self-aware can help you feel more mindful. You could try breathing exercises, guided meditation, yoga, journaling, therapy, talking to a friend about how you feel, or taking a few minutes to reflect on the day before falling asleep.

AVOID THE "COMPARISON TRAP"

You are scrolling through *Instagram* and see someone's charming New York City apartment, another person's two-week trip to Paris, a breathtaking wedding, someone's cool urban office, and cute couple photo after cute couple photo. It may feel like everyone has their life together…except you. You might want some of those things and feel jealous.

You are experiencing the social comparison theory, which says that one way people determine their personal and professional self-worth is by comparing themselves to other people. It can lead to lower self-esteem, feeling sad, and always feeling like you aren't good enough or your current situation isn't good enough.

Don't Compare Your Life to Someone Else's Highlight Reel

One of the main triggers of social comparison is social media. You see people's lives on *Instagram*, *Snapchat*, *Facebook*, *Twitter*, and *LinkedIn*, but you are only looking at carefully curated pieces that they choose to share. People rarely share the mistakes, heartbreak, family stress, jobs or promotions they *didn't* get, and all the messy moments. Social media is a highlight reel; it isn't the real story. What if you curated your top moments from the year—what would they look like? Think about your best moments as you look at other people's.

If you realize that your feelings of envy and feeling less-than spike when you check social media, try these ideas:

- Unfollow people who regularly make you feel bad
- Limit yourself to fifteen minutes a day of scrolling
- Take a social media detox for a month and see how you feel

Think about Your Intentions

Have you ever done something because you thought other people would be impressed and you wanted their approval? If you find yourself thinking that you "should" do something, pause and think about if it is actually something *you* want. When you think about what you "should" do, you are often thinking about external motivations for doing something, like your parents' or friend's approval or that your job will sound impressive when you talk about it at your five-year reunion or a cocktail party…even though you'll actually be miserable because the job doesn't play to any of your strengths and you think the work is boring.

Focus On What You Have

When you compare yourself to someone else, you are thinking about what they have that you don't. Instead, think about what you have, what makes you happy, and what makes you grateful. Take out your journal and write a list of things that you are happy about, things you've accomplished and are proud of, people who make you feel supported, and things that are going well in your life. You'll be happier if you focus on what you have, not what you want.

Then, write down what success means to you, because it might not mean the same thing right now (or ever) as it does to the people you follow on social media or your friends. Think about your priorities, values, and what you want in your personal and professional life. Write down times that you felt most proud of yourself, accomplished, energized, and happy.

Use Envy As a Motivator

If you find that you are jealous about something you actually want and care about, like being in a serious relationship, getting a promotion, or moving out of your parents' home and into an apartment, use that feeling as a motivator. Instead of waiting for something to happen, remind yourself of your five-year plan and check in on your progress in each area, then take steps to move them forward. Sign up for dating apps or go to more events where you might meet someone in person. Put more energy into your work and identify ways you can create even more value. Look at your budget and see how you can save or earn more money so you can move out sooner.

If you encounter people you admire who have achieved things you would like to achieve, figure out how they got where they are now. Ask people for advice if you have specific questions and learn from them.

TREAT YOUR MENTAL HEALTH AS SERIOUSLY AS YOUR PHYSICAL HEALTH

Mental health and therapy is sometimes stigmatized, and that can keep people from asking for help, knowing how to find it, or recognizing when it may be necessary.

Two of the most common mental health conditions are depression and anxiety. Depression is different than being sad. Everyone feels sad sometimes, and everyone encounters circumstances that make them sad for a while. But when sadness persists and affects your daily life, it could be a sign of something more serious. Some signs of depression are persistent sadness, loss of interest in things you used to find fun, a loss of energy, feeling guilty or worthless, having difficulty concentrating and doing work that used to be easy, or even thoughts of death or suicide, according to the American Psychiatric Association.

Likewise, anxiety is not just feeling stressed. There are different types of anxiety disorders, but one of the most common is generalized anxiety disorder. Symptoms include persistent and excessive worries that interfere with day-to-day life, restlessness, difficulty concentrating, trouble sleeping, and feeling on edge, according to the American Psychiatric Association. Like with depression, anxiety interferes with day-to-day life.

If symptoms of either of these conditions sound familiar, make it a priority to speak to a mental health professional.

Types of Mental Health Professionals

People who haven't had much experience with mental health professionals can be confused by the terminology associated with them. Here's a primer so you understand who's who.

- **Psychiatrists** are doctors who went to medical school and completed a residency and are able to prescribe medication if they think it would be helpful. Psychiatrists can make a diagnosis and help create a treatment plan by running psychological tests and lab tests and looking at someone's medical history, genetics, and other data.
- **Psychologists** are not medical doctors, but they need to go through training to be able to practice.

Psychiatrists and psychologists can both do psychotherapy, which can be helpful. You can see both: Visit a psychologist for psychotherapy and a psychiatrist to prescribe or monitor medication if they think it would help alleviate symptoms.

If you think therapy might be helpful for you, learn more about the types available to you. There are many branches, but two main types of psychotherapy are psychodynamic therapy and cognitive behavioral therapy (CBT).

Psychodynamic Therapy

When you imagine someone lying on a couch talking to a therapist who is jotting down notes, you are thinking of psychodynamic therapy. The therapist listens to the person talk about their life, often from early childhood to the present day, and can help identify patterns or events that might be contributing to current difficulties.

These therapists will often meet with people once a week for a few months or even years. The goal is to have deep conversations that help people understand strengths and weaknesses and behavioral patterns—and to identify coping mechanisms. Research has shown that psychodynamic therapy is valuable for people because it offers a safe space to talk freely without judgment. This type of therapy can be expensive because appointments are typically scheduled regularly, but your health insurance plan might cover part of the cost.

Cognitive Behavioral Therapy

Cognitive behavioral therapy (CBT) focuses on a specific problem to help people change their thought patterns. CBT can help with phobias, addictions, depression, and anxiety and is usually a short-term treatment that helps people understand their feelings and develop specific coping mechanisms.

If someone experiences low self-esteem, the therapist might help with identifying negative thoughts, reversing misperceptions, thinking positively, and identifying solutions for increasing confidence. It is a very structured and goal-oriented type of treatment.

Finding a Therapist

Your general practitioner can help you decide what type of mental health professional to see and can explain which treatment method might be more helpful for you. Call to ask if the recommended provider takes your insurance or look on various online resources like *GoodTherapy, Zocdoc, Psychology Today*, or your insurance provider's website.

Unfortunately, plans with high-deductible payments might not pay a copay for therapy until your deductible has been met, and therapy can be expensive. That shouldn't dissuade you from getting the help you need, though. Look for alternative solutions, like going to group therapy and support groups, or using a therapy app like Talkspace or BetterHelp.

Points to Remember

- Set boundaries around work so you can enjoy your time away from the office.

- Schedule time to relax just like you would any other priority. Spend the time doing something you enjoy, like a hobby.

- Resilience will help you get through difficult times in your life.

- Healthy coping mechanisms give you the power to process tough emotions in a productive way.

- There is always a way to get help, and you are never alone.

Chapter 12

Take Care of Your Spiritual Health

Spirituality is very personal, and everyone has different spiritual beliefs. For some, it could be tied to faith in God or another higher power. Others find spirituality in self-care practices like practicing meditation and yoga. The great thing about spirituality is that you can try new things and incorporate many types of spiritual practices into your life throughout the next five years. Did any of your goals that you listed in Chapter 1 address spirituality? Now is the time to think about them. In this chapter, you'll learn spirituality practices you can try and how to find your purpose and develop it.

ESTABLISH WHAT SPIRITUALITY MEANS TO YOU

Spirituality offers many benefits. It can:

- Help you feel calmer, more centered, and more mindful.
- Decrease anxiety.
- Make you feel happier.
- Give you a sense of community and make you feel less alone (either because you have faith in a religious sense or because you've found people with similar interests).
- Guide you to develop your personal values and morals and understand your emotions. Whether you choose religion, meditation, affirmations, gratitude, service, or a combination, find something (or a few things) that help you find a sense of peace...even if it's just for fifteen minutes at a time.

TRY THESE EVERYDAY WAYS TO BE SPIRITUAL

You can find spirituality in a number of outlets.

Practice Yoga

Yoga is an exercise for your mind and body that's thousands of years old. It often incorporates breathing exercises, movement, poses, and meditation. Yoga can decrease stress and anxiety, help reduce chronic pain, increase flexibility and balance, improve breathing and strength, and promote self-awareness, among other benefits. There are yoga mantras that you can repeat to increase mindfulness and focus on the emotion you want to feel, like peace, love, joy, and strength.

Go to Religious Services

Whether you grew up going to religious services once a week, a few times a year, or never, you can start making it part of your life now. You may find a new community filled with like-minded people who are supportive and caring and share similar values. You could read religious texts and apply the stories and lessons to your own life.

You can learn about personal values, kindness, life and death, community, and faith from visiting places of worship that are unfamiliar to you. It can be eye-opening to see the differences even within branches of the same religion.

Volunteer in Your Community

Find a cause that matters to you and a way that you can give back. You could tutor kids in math, foster cats and dogs so they have a loving home, spend time with the elderly who might not have family nearby, or help a high school student through the college application process. The main goal of volunteering is to help others, but, as an added bonus, you are also enriching your life. It gives you a sense of purpose, puts your own life and worries in perspective, and makes you happy.

Start a Meditation Practice

Meditation is a great way to release stress and anxiety, relax, and practice being in the present moment. It helps you gain awareness of your feelings and emotions, find clarity, and feel calm. People have been meditating for thousands of years, and there is a wide variety of types of meditation practice. If you are just getting started, it can be helpful to do the guided meditations offered in an app like Calm or Headspace.

Meditating for as little as five minutes a day can help you feel calmer and more self-aware and more compassionate and empathetic. You can fit five minutes of meditation into your day: Take a few minutes to meditate in the shower, during your commute, before you get out of bed in the morning, or before you fall asleep at night.

Focus On Gratitude

The simple act of thinking about what you are grateful for can improve your physical and mental health. A gratitude practice can make you happier and more resilient and confident.

Make it a daily habit to write down five things that you are grateful for in the moment. It can help you have a more positive and optimistic outlook on life and, as an added bonus, you can look back through your journal and reread what you wrote to feel better when you are having a bad day.

Look for Silver Linings

When bad things happen, it can be hard to imagine that anything good could possibly come from the situation. Still, try to look for the silver lining. Believe that something good can come from almost any bad situation. Looking for the good can help you be resilient as you try to move forward.

Spend Time in Nature

Go for a hike, take a long walk, garden, or go for a run. Get outside and connect with nature. Cycling classes and treadmills are great, especially on rainy or cold days, but try to also run, walk, or bike outdoors. Spending time in nature can improve your physical and mental health. Bring some nature inside by keeping a plant on your desk at work and in your home. Plants can decrease your stress, improve your air quality, and make your space more beautiful. It is fun to have something to take care of every day.

Pray

Prayer is very personal. You may have grown up praying to God every night before bed, or you might never have prayed before. You could pray to a higher power for "traditional" things, like your family's health and happiness or a job you really want, but you can also say prayers to show gratitude. You could use prayer as a personal time to reflect on what you hope for yourself and others and what makes you grateful. Prayer can be religious or it can be a time for personal self-reflection. It is up to you.

Do a Good Deed

Volunteering and making philanthropic donations are great ways to get in touch with your spiritual side, but there are also smaller actions you can take to help your friends, family, and community. Spirituality is about finding meaning and personal values, and helping others gives you a sense of purpose and connection.

Challenge yourself to doing a small good deed every day or once a week. It could be checking in on a friend because you know she is going through a hard time, calling a parent or grandparent just to say hello, bringing a bag of groceries to a local food bank, cleaning out your closet and donating clothing, donating school supplies at back-to-school season, taking a CPR class, offering to babysit to help a family member or friend, sending someone flowers out of the blue, playing with puppies at an animal shelter, or complimenting someone. The possibilities are endless!

Practice Forgiveness

Forgiveness is a core theme of many spiritual practices. It is normal to get angry with other people and to be mad at yourself. It can be hard to forgive people when they hurt your feelings or to forgive yourself when you make a mistake. But it's worth the effort—it will make you happier. Forgiveness can improve mental health and self-esteem; lead to healthier relationships; and decrease anxiety, stress, hostility, and symptoms of depression.

If you hurt someone else's feelings, even unintentionally, apologize sincerely. It's the first step to mending the relationship. You can't control other people's reactions, only your own. The person might not forgive you, but you will be able to learn from the situation and move on knowing you tried to remedy it.

Forgiving yourself and others is beneficial for you. You need to forgive yourself and other people to get rid of the negative feelings like resentment, anger, and sadness, which can have an impact on your mental and physical health. First, it's helpful to take time to process your emotions and, if it involves someone else, talk about how you feel. Forgiveness doesn't mean you forget what happened; it just means you let go of the past and move forward. It could mean that you both move on and end the relationship but that you've forgiven each other first, so the anger starts to subside.

You might find that you are harder on yourself than other people and that it's harder to forgive yourself when you think you made a mistake. Take responsibility for your actions, process your emotions including feeling sad or sorry, make amends if you hurt someone, then focus on what you learned and what you will do differently next time.

FOCUS ON YOUR PERSONAL VALUES

If you're still not sure how to practice spirituality, look inward. Think about the personal values that are important to you, like kindness, friendship, honesty, love, loyalty, motivation, and ambition. Conduct yourself according to your personal values and surround yourself with people who have a similar moral compass.

Live by the Golden Rule: Treat others how you want to be treated. Write down your top five personal values, what they mean to you, and ways you can continue to live your values.

— TO DO —
FIND YOUR PURPOSE AND NOURISH IT

Finding a sense of meaning and purpose is one of the core themes of spirituality. The Japanese concept *ikigai* is the belief that everyone has a purpose in life. As research for their book *Ikigai: The Japanese Secret to a Long and Healthy Life*, authors Francesc Miralles and Héctor García spoke with the residents of the Japanese village with one of the highest percentage of 100-year-olds in the world, who told them that finding *ikigai* leads to a longer and happier life. "Having a strong sense of *ikigai*—the place where passion, mission, vocation, and profession intersect—means that each day is infused with meaning," they wrote. *Ikigai* is personal: Each person has a different *ikigai* based on her personal values, goals, and interests. It shows how you can take what you care about, what you are good at, and the value you provide to find your purpose. To find your *ikigai*, work through the following questions in your journal.

Step 1: Determine What You Are Passionate About
Think about what makes you passionate. What classes or extracurriculars made you feel excited, motivated, and purposeful? Maybe it was being president of your sorority because you realized you like leadership positions and helping to create a supportive community of like-minded people. Maybe it was working as a student emergency medical technician because you like taking care of people when they are feeling at their worst. Write the answers to these questions in your journal:

- What do I care about?
- What did I enjoy doing when I was a child?
- What makes me feel energized and motivated?

continued on next page

Step 2: Figure Out What You Love to Do

What work makes you feel happy? There is the common saying "Do what you love, and you'll never work another day in your life." That's not quite true because every job has some aspects that are boring or frustrating, but if you can find something you enjoy 90 percent of the time, you will be happy. Write the answers to these questions:

- What work makes me happy?
- What would I do for work if money weren't a factor?
- What type of work keeps me from looking at the clock every five minutes?
- What am I good at?

Now think about your strengths. What are the top five things you are really good at? Think of both hard skills such as math, writing, coding, and research, and soft skills such as teamwork, enthusiasm, optimism, and effective communication. Think of the positive feedback you've received in the past and the type of work that has made you the most proud. Write the answers to these questions:

- What are my top five hard skills?
- What are my top five soft skills?
- What are patterns in the positive feedback I've been given?
- What type of work has made me feel the most proud?

Step 3: Think about What You Can Contribute to the World

Now think about ways you can use your unique combination of strengths to provide the biggest benefit to others. If you are compassionate, a problem-solver, calm under pressure, driven, logical, and knowledgeable about medicine, you would be able to help people as a doctor or nurse. Write the answers to these questions:

- How can I provide the most value to other people?
- What value do I want to provide?
- How can I make a difference?

Step 4: Consider What You Can Get Paid For

Think about the types of jobs that match your interests, unique skill set, and the value you want to provide to other people. Read job postings to find the type of work that appeals to you. Write the answers to these questions:

- What industries match my skill sets and interests?
- What roles match my skill sets and interests?

The intersection of all your answers is your *ikigai*—your purpose. If you use your strengths, add value to other people's lives, and enjoy what you do 90 percent of the time, you'll be more fulfilled, driven, and motivated to work hard because you are working toward a greater good.

JOIN A COMMUNITY

Spirituality is often more meaningful when you join a supportive and loving community of people who share similar beliefs and values. It doesn't have to mean belonging to one place of worship and attending religious services every week, although many people find their community that way. You can find a community anywhere.

Meditation or Yoga Class

There are meditation and yoga classes and studios around the world where you can find a community of people committed to spirituality, mindfulness, self-awareness, and growth. Group meditation can help people feel less lonely, more committed to meditating regularly, and more connected, and it can lead to a deeper practice, according to Deepak Chopra, a world-renowned expert in integrative medicine and personal transformation. Yoga class can do the same. You don't have to be part of a large group; you can also find a few friends who like to meditate or do yoga and make a date.

Volunteer Programs

There are countless ways you can volunteer in your community, some of which have been mentioned. You can help people or animals in need, and volunteering is beneficial for your spiritual and mental health. Volunteering helps you connect, can decrease stress and symptoms of depression, and can increase a sense of meaning and purpose. Part of spirituality is connection with other people. You will feel a sense of connection if you volunteer one-on-one, but volunteering with a like-minded group of people who care about similar things can help you feel a stronger connection with the community you've created for yourself.

Community Center

Many neighborhoods have community centers you can join to take classes, meet people, attend events, and make friends. Some community centers have a religious affiliation, but often you do not have to be a member of the religion to enjoy the services the center provides, which might be fitness, cooking, or art classes, and a variety of social events. Joining a community center can be a great way to meet twentysomethings and make new friends—or find love.

Place of Worship

If you are religious, it can be valuable to join a place of worship. Whether you go to services every week, once a month, or a handful of times a year, it will help you build your community and share your spirituality with like-minded people. Many places of worship have classes you can take to feel more connected to your religion and to learn from other people in your religious community.

Points to Remember

- There are many different types of spirituality practices. Find what works best for you.

- Your personal values serve as a moral compass for all your decisions.

- Find ways to integrate spirituality practices into your day-to-day life from five-minute meditations to doing a good deed a day.

- Spirituality will help you find purpose throughout the next five years and the rest of your life.

Part 4

RELATIONSHIPS

This part will help you find your "people": the ones who encourage you and love you. The good days, and even the bad ones, are better when you have close relationships with people who support you and always know the right thing to say or when to just listen. You might have met some of your "people" in college, but now that you've graduated, you're no longer living steps away from all your closest friends. Some of you might have met your partner in college, and some might be navigating a dating scene where you no longer meet someone in class or activities on campus. You might be living at home again or living in a new city with roommates you just met. In this part, you'll work on nurturing your relationships and expanding your support system, no matter where you are right now or where you'll be throughout the next five years.

Chapter 13
Develop Your Family Relationships

Now that you're entering a new phase of your life, all of your relationships will be changing, including your relationships with family members. This chapter will help you set boundaries, decide which advice to take, and be supportive. It will discuss new family relationships like stepsiblings, stepparents, brothers- and sisters-in-laws, and your own in-laws.

MANAGE YOUR CHANGING RELATIONSHIP WITH YOUR PARENTS

Your relationship with your parents naturally changes over time, and, as you get older, you will rely on them less than you did when you were younger. (And, as your parents get older, the roles may reverse and they may rely on you more.) Not everyone has a close relationship with their parents, but if you do, you'll likely notice changes now that you're out of college.

You're More Independent, but You Still Need Them

When you were younger, you relied on your parents for everything. But now you are paying your bills, living on your own (or will be soon), and making your own decisions.

Even though you are more independent in a lot of ways, you can still rely on your parents for advice and support. The five years after college present many new situations: You're working full-time, dating or becoming more serious with a current partner, and meeting new friends and coworkers. Your parents have been through this transition before. While they don't have all the answers (and probably made their fair share of mistakes), they may have some valuable advice: Reach out for help. They may have more experience with certain things like taxes or investing, and they might be able to give you actionable advice.

Set Boundaries

Every healthy relationship has some boundaries, and the one with your parents is no different. You are an adult, but your parents might have a difficult time seeing you as one and not the baby, kid, and teenager they lived with for eighteen years. They might ask lots of questions or offer unwanted advice. If that happens, gently set up boundaries. You can make certain topics off-limits, including politics and questions like "Have you met anyone yet," "Are you getting engaged," or "When will you give me grandkids already?" Try saying something like "We want to get married and have kids someday, but we aren't ready for that step in our relationship yet. We'll let you know when we are planning to get engaged, but in the meantime please stop asking about it whenever I call." Parents may try to make all your decisions for you, from where you live to where you work to whom you date to how you spend your money. You could say something like "I thought about what you said about living out here being cheaper, Mom, but living in the city is a better choice for me right now because my commute is so much shorter and it's easier to meet up with my friends after work and on weekends. I have two roommates, so I'm not spending more than I can afford on rent." Listen to your parents' advice and, if you agree, take it, but at the end of the day you are paying your own bills now and it's really your decision.

Don't Seek Their Approval

Asking for or listening to advice from your parents is one thing, but feeling like they have to sign off on every decision you make is taking things too far. Take the suggestions that you truly believe are good ones, but make your own decisions. You might consciously or unconsciously seek your parents' approval on everything from whether to take a "prestigious" job (which they can brag about), to whether you live in the same state or a ten-minute drive away, to the person you choose to date. Before you make a decision, ask yourself if you are truly making it because it's what *you* want and what is best for *you*, or if your decision is motivated by what you think you "should" do or your parents' expectations and hopes for you.

TO DO

CONSIDER...SHOULD YOU TAKE THE ADVICE?

You don't have to take all the advice people give. Ask yourself these questions before you make a decision and listen to your intuition when you consider the answers:

- Is this person an expert or someone whose opinion I trust?
- Has previous advice from them been helpful?
- Does this person understand my situation? Did they listen to me?
- Do I agree with the advice?

Accept Them for Who They Are

When you're young, you might think your parents are nearly perfect. As you mature, you realize that your parents are human, just like you. They make mistakes and have flaws. Now is a good time to accept them for who they are, not the "perfect" people you might have once thought. It will help you learn to see everyone objectively and be more accepting of other people because you realize it's okay for people to have some flaws and make mistakes—no one is perfect. It will also help you be more accepting of yourself because everyone is trying their best and figuring it out along the way.

You Become Their Caregiver

As your parents get older, they may turn to you to for help. This help could be relatively minor, like setting up their new iPad, or it could be more serious, like dealing with their health concerns. Start thinking about how you can check on them to see if they need help. If you live far away, call periodically and ask some specific questions about how things are going with their health or maintaining their house. If you live nearby, stop by in person sometimes to have dinner or offer to come with them to important doctor appointments.

If their health or home situation deteriorates, you might need to have honest conversations about their health and finances. If you have siblings, include them in the conversation so you can all support each other and your parents. These conversations can be difficult, so look for professional resources, like the AARP website. Talk about these things early so you have plenty of time to support their needs and goals.

Move On If Need Be

If you don't have a good relationship with your parents or other family members, or any, now might be a good time to build a new family. Invite friends to holiday celebrations and create new traditions.

Someday, you can create a new family of your own, if you want. Make up for what you think you missed and wish you had growing up, and be that loving partner and parent for your family.

NURTURE RELATIONSHIPS WITH EXTENDED FAMILY

If you're lucky, you have a close extended family made up of cousins, aunts and uncles, and grandparents. Sometimes you may get on each other's nerves, and you might have certain topics that are off-limits, but you love them and they provide a strong support system that you trust and rely on. If you don't, it's never too late to try to forge a closer bond. You can learn something from another generation or even a cousin who is a few years older. They've been with you throughout your life, so they "get it" in a way that a newer friend might not, and you don't have to explain the long backstory every time you ask for advice or tell a story. If you don't have siblings, you can have a similar relationship with your cousins...and it will make Thanksgiving and other family events more fun!

Make Plans Outside of Family Events

Do you have any cousins or aunts and uncles that you only see at holidays and other family events? Make plans to get together in one-on-one settings or smaller groups outside of family gatherings so you can have meaningful conversations in between holidays.

There's no substitute for meaningful interactions offline: Get together with your cousins, write letters to your aunt, and set up phone dates to catch up with your grandmother. Use any social media posts your family make as a reminder to check in and see how they are doing offline.

Be There for Them When They Need You

You should be able to rely on your family, and vice versa. Turn to them when you need a night away when things have gotten tense with your roommates, and offer them your couch if they're visiting your town for a night. Be supportive in return, and offer to help, even when they don't ask.

Reach Out and Check In with Older Family Members

Call just to say hello and see how your family members are doing—especially older ones. If you still have grandparents and great-aunts and -uncles, call more frequently and visit when you can. Getting older can be lonely, and it can be hard to transition to being dependent on other people. They may not ask for help or company because they don't want to burden you or be vulnerable. If you live nearby, stop by and visit, offer to come over to cook dinner for them, bring groceries, or run errands.

WELCOME NEW FAMILY MEMBERS

There are different kinds of family dynamics, especially when divorce, remarriage, stepsiblings, and new younger siblings are involved. Even though you graduated college, your younger sibling or stepsibling might be graduating from preschool. Or maybe you have a very serious significant other and are becoming closer with their family, or you just got married and have in-laws now.

Stepparents (or Parents' Partners)

If your parents remarry, are in new relationships, or are starting to date again, you may have to figure out the relationship you want to have with the person who might be in their life forever or just for a few months. You'll probably handle the situation differently depending on the specifics:

- If your parents remarry when you are young, you might live in the same house as this person for part or all of the time. You might become so close that they feel like another parent.
- If you're an adult when this person enters your life, you might initially feel less of a connection. If you only see them every so often, it might feel like more of a relationship you have with a distant family member. You are kind to them and talk when you see them, but you don't have a strong bond.
- If you're an adult and a parent's significant other ends up staying around long-term, you might choose to make more of an effort to create a stronger connection. You might see exactly what your parent sees in them and realize that you really get along. If not, just be cordial and happy your parent found someone they care about.

As your parents get older, you'll probably be grateful that they have a companion in their life—someone they love and trust who is emotionally supportive and there for them—so keep an open mind.

New Siblings and Stepsiblings

Similarly, when you grow up in the same house with your siblings or stepsiblings, you are bound to have a closer relationship than you will if you have never lived under the same roof. Be open to the possibility that you will be able to have a close relationship and that they will become a friend or confidant if you are close in age. If you are more than a decade older, you may enjoy watching your much younger sibling grow up, cheering on the sidelines of their soccer games, and celebrating their high school graduation. As adults, you may become more like friends as the age gap matters less.

Sometimes, difficult feelings can come up with stepsiblings. Even if you know your parents love you unconditionally, you may still feel "replaced" by stepsiblings and much younger siblings or jealous of their relationship with your parent, either consciously or unconsciously.

If something bothers you, have an honest and open conversation about it with your parent or explain your feelings to a therapist. If you feel comfortable, try to spend more time with your stepsiblings, either in person or by catching up with a phone call more frequently.

Your In-Laws

Whether you are married or in a serious relationship, or your siblings are married and you have brothers- and sisters-in-law, the in-law dynamic is a new one for you to manage. When you gain new family members, it can be amazing or challenging…or a combination of both.

Ideally, you'll have a close relationship with your partner's family and enjoy what they bring to your life—like family traditions you can join or a sister or brother if you don't have one already.

If you don't, be polite and cordial when you see them at the inevitable countless family events you'll both attend throughout the years.

Points to Remember

- Your relationship with your parents will grow and mature at this phase of your life. Enjoy these changes, but remember to live your life how you want to, not to meet their expectations.

- Try to deepen your connection to extended family members and welcome people who are new to your family.

- Blended families can be challenging at times, but they can provide opportunities for close relationships and new traditions.

- If your family isn't fulfilling you, create your own family with friends whose company you enjoy.

Chapter 14

Manage Your Social Life

Making and maintaining friends in college is relatively easy because you meet many people, many of whom share similar interests. You might instantly become friends with roommates or people you sit next to in class or share hobbies with, like the newspaper, ultimate Frisbee team, or a sorority or fraternity. Plus, socializing is hassle-free—you can see your friends every day.

Once you graduate, things change quite a bit—the friendships you have will grow, and you will meet new people. You have to put in a bit more effort to make new friends after graduation, but it's worth it to have a social life that helps you thrive. This chapter will cover how to make friends outside of a school setting, recognize types of friendships to have in your circle, have tough conversations respectfully, and deal with friendships that change in unexpected ways.

MAKE NEW FRIENDS

Making new friends post-college is rewarding. You're a little older and wiser, and you probably have an even better idea of the type of person you get along with well. You might be living in a new place with new people, so you are able to meet a more diverse group than those you went to high school or college with, or you might be on the lookout for a specific type of friend, like someone to run half-marathons with or someone who enjoys your other hobbies.

Meet Friends of Friends

If you are moving to a new city where you don't have a support system yet, ask your friends or family members to introduce you to people they know who live there. That way, you'll meet people who have been "preapproved." You'll probably have similar values and personality traits since you share friends in common. Get together with the friend of a friend and, if you hit it off, ask if you could meet their friends and go to group gatherings like birthday parties or movie nights.

Join Organizations

Meet people with similar interests and hobbies by joining community centers, volunteer groups, alumni groups, or sports leagues. You're likely to find many fun groups of twenty- and thirtysomethings who are navigating the first few years out of college and are looking to meet new people. If you have specific interests, look for classes or groups so you can get to know people who share similar hobbies like photography, hiking, cooking, or running.

Accept All the Invitations You Get

It can be tempting to sit on your couch and watch Netflix when your social circle is a bit thin, but try to push out of your comfort zone when you get the chance. Parties and group events are a great way to meet a lot of new people at once, make new friends, and maybe even find love. If you're naturally outgoing, this shouldn't be too difficult.

If you are going to a big but casual get-together like a birthday party or housewarming party and you don't know anyone other than the guest of honor, ask if you can bring a friend or your partner along. (Formal events like weddings are totally different—don't ask to bring a "plus one" if it wasn't offered.) Be sure you and whomever you bring make an effort to join conversations and meet people.

If you're more introverted, it can be intimidating to go to social events. You might be nervous about introducing yourself or keeping up the momentum of the conversation if you find that you don't seem to have too much to talk about and don't have much in common other than the fact that you are both at the same event. Instead of talking one-on-one, introduce yourself to a group of people who are chatting so you don't feel pressured to be the person who has to keep the conversation going. If you are having trouble finding a conversation to join, have some go-to questions or conversation topics to bring up if the conversation starts to stall, like asking for recommendations of good restaurants, museums, or things to do and see in the city. People like sharing recommendations, and you are bound to gather some good intel.

Be Brave: Make the First Move

No matter where you end up meeting a potential friend, reach out and try to build a friendship. Ask for her number and text to get together for coffee or drinks. It might feel uncomfortable at first, but give it a shot. Worst case, the person declines, but the best-case scenario is that you have a great time and become friends.

Ten Types of Friendships Everyone Should Have

Be on the lookout for these types of friends, and know that one person can fit into a few of the categories!

- **A cheerleader**: This person helps you recognize your accomplishments and all of your great qualities and always helps you feel better when you feel down or insecure. They will talk you up to other people, so it's especially great if you have a cheerleader at work or when you are meeting new people.
- **A work friend**: This person makes the workday infinitely better. You have someone to laugh with, get coffee with, ask for advice, and get helpful feedback from on projects.
- **A confidant**: This is someone you know you can call at 3 a.m. and put down as your emergency contact. It's someone you tell everything to and know you can confide in because they are not judgmental and always know the right thing to say. When something great or lousy happens, they are always one of the first people you want to tell.
- **A motivator**: This is someone who encourages you to be the best version of yourself. They help you feel more confident and motivate you to apply for a promotion, stick to your financial goals, or whatever it is you want to accomplish. They help you realize you can do it and support you every step of the way.
- **A connector**: This person seems to know everyone, and they love to help their friends connect and get to know each other.

They love to throw events or invite a group of people to lunch or dinner, so you always end up meeting new people when you are with them.

- **An adventurer**: This person enjoys doing similar activities as you and is always up for doing something fun and different like going to a trapeze class, taking an improv class, visiting a museum, cooking an elaborate dinner, or running a race. When you want to try something new and fun, they are one of the first people you call!

- **An energizer**: You feel like you've just had a venti coffee when you are with them. They are so enthusiastic and optimistic, and you always feel better after spending time with them.

- **A coach**: This person helps you reach your goal, whether they are literally coaching you for your first half-marathon and helping you see yourself as a "runner," helping you reach your goals at work, or giving you valuable advice on everything from dating to decorating your apartment. They listen to your dreams and goals and give you the support and encouragement to reach them—even if it is as simple as sending a quick message when they see an *Instagram* story of you out on a run or working on your novel.

- **A comedian**: This person makes you laugh so hard you cry and is both fun and funny. They remind you to lighten up, be playful, and joke around.

- **A big sibling:** This person might actually be a sibling, or is someone who feels like one. They love you, are proud of you, encourage you, and often have great advice because they have been through some of the things you are experiencing.

BE AN EVEN BETTER FRIEND

Friendships change, and you might need to offer a friend support in a way that's new to you. This section will walk you through some ways to deepen your friendships.

Listen Actively

One of the most important components of any relationship is to be an active listener. An active listener is empathetic and caring. Fully concentrate on what someone's saying, ask questions, be nonjudgmental, and wait before giving advice. Active listening shows that you care, gives people an opportunity to come to their own decisions or gain clarity from talking freely, and leads to vulnerability and more meaningful conversations. If someone asks for your advice, you'll be well equipped to answer since you've listened so attentively.

Your friend may not expect or want you to try to "fix" what they are going through, and sometimes there may be no easy solution anyway. However, active listening will help people come to their own conclusions.

Try repeating back what the person says in your own words to show that you are listening and that you understand their perspective. Then ask follow-up questions to help them discover their own advice before you give yours.

Share Mistakes You've Made

It is valuable to be honest and vulnerable with your friend about the mistakes you've made and the things you'd do differently. You've learned from your mistakes and missteps, so why not pass on that knowledge to your friends? Sometimes people are afraid of being vulnerable and honest, but it makes your friendship stronger, so give it a try.

Give Them Advice (but Don't Expect Them to Take It)

If your friend asks you for advice, try to gauge what they really want before you dive in too deeply. Sometimes people ask for advice when they're actually seeking confirmation that they made a good decision, or want your support so they feel more secure about having made a choice.

If you have a friend dealing with an especially difficult issue (such as a breakup, getting laid off, or a sick parent), remember that you don't have to fix their problem to be a supportive friend. Be an empathetic, active listener and follow up later and ask them how they are doing.

If they really do want your advice, try these alternatives to saying "You should do XXX." You could say "Well, if it were me, I would..." or say "I'm sure you know what's best, but since you asked me, I'd do XXX," or "In my experience, XXX." Better yet, ask questions that help them come to their own conclusions.

After you give advice, step back and see how things unfold. Your friend might go in a different direction than you suggested. If that happens, don't feel hurt. You might have given your friend the confidence to make their own decision, and that's important too. Even if you think the decision was "wrong," be sure to avoid statements like "I told you so" or "You should've taken my advice."

HANDLE TOUGH CONVERSATIONS

If you have a disagreement with a friend or something is hurting your feelings, talk about it so you can move forward. Tough conversations aren't fun; they're stressful, unpredictable, and unpleasant. Instead of focusing on the negative aspects of the conversation, think about the positive outcomes that may result. You might be able to resolve a disagreement, apologize if you're in the wrong, or stand up for yourself.

It's better to have a difficult conversation as soon as possible rather than waiting for it to get worse. Though it's tempting to avoid bringing up tough topics, the issues are unlikely to get resolved on their own and could get increasingly worse until one of you hits a breaking point. Waiting can be unfair to the other person—they might not even know that you are upset! Why waste time if the issue could have been resolved weeks ago?

Prepare for the Conversation

Preparing for a conversation is a smart idea for many reasons. First, it gives both people time to cool down and avoid saying something regrettable in the heat of the moment. It allows you to organize your thoughts and determine what your goals are for the conversation.

Let's say you are upset with a friend because the last few times you've tried to make plans, she has either canceled last minute, not texted you back to choose a time and place, or arrived half an hour late. Before you talk to the friend, ask yourself why that behavior bothered you and how it made you feel. Perhaps you feel like they don't value your friendship or your time and may even be waiting for a better invitation, and it hurt your feelings.

Other times, you might know that you are upset but not be able to articulate your emotions quite yet. If that's the case, talk about how you are feeling with a friend, family member, or partner in advance so you gain clarity about how you feel and what you want to say.

Planning ahead gives you time to think of what your intention is for the conversation. The goal might be to resolve a disagreement, apologize and each take responsibility for the situation, and, ultimately, move forward. Sharing your intention is a productive way to begin the conversation. You could start by saying something like "I really value our friendship and want to talk about something that upset me. I want to hear your perspective."

TO DO

TRY JOURNALING PROMPTS TO PREPARE FOR A TOUGH CONVERSATION

Journaling can help you find clarity in how you're feeling so you are better able to communicate that in the conversation. Take a few minutes to answer these questions in your journal before a tough conversation.

- Why am I upset?
- How does the behavior or situation make me feel?
- What do I hope to gain from this conversation?
- What is the other person's perspective?
- How can I make the conversation positive instead of feeling like an attack?
- How can I say this using "I" language (like "I feel...")?
- How can I make my points specific? Are there specific instances that I should reference?
- How can I avoid blame or criticism?
- What is the best possible outcome of having this conversation?
- What are some possible resolutions?

Describe How You Feel

When you bring up something that is upsetting you, describe a specific instance and how it made you feel. People can't read your mind, and even if you think they should realize that you are upset, they might genuinely not know. It's easier for the other person to understand where you are coming from if they have an example of why you are upset, which is another reason it's helpful to say something sooner rather than later.

You could say something like "The last few times we've tried to make plans, I felt like you ignored my text messages about finalizing a plan, canceled last minute, or showed up late. I understand that things come up, but it makes me feel like you don't want to get together."

Don't Blame the Other Person

Frame the conversation as your point of view, not a fact. Instead of using "you" language that instantly places blame, use "I" language and say how you feel. It gives you a chance to share your perspective, invites their response, and shifts the tone from accusatory and blame-based to cooperative. Continue talking about specific behaviors and instances, but instead of saying something definitive such as "You are disrespectful of my time," try something like "I feel like lately I've been the one to reach out to make plans and that you've had to cancel last minute. It makes me feel like you aren't as invested in our friendship. I understand that you might be busy, but I wanted to let you know how I feel."

Listen to and Acknowledge the Other Person's Feelings

Give the other person a chance to respond and explain how they feel. In the case of the friend who cancels plans, maybe they apologize and say that they've been working late and don't have a lot of control over their schedule right now.

Let them share their perspective. Truly listen and acknowledge their feelings. Ask questions if it will help you better understand their perspective, even if you'd rather smile and nod so the conversation is over faster. You might learn that you've hurt the other person's feelings at some point too, at which point you can apologize.

Don't Be Competitive

Instead of treating a tough conversation like a chess game and thinking about your next move or how you'll "win," think about the end goal you planned. It's not about having a winner; it's about resolving an issue and moving forward. Don't treat it as a competition or be too stubborn to compromise. Try not to bring up old issues from the past because it can understandably seem like you've been keeping score, which can put people on edge.

Come Up with a Resolution

The goal of a tough conversation is to make things better. Try to come up with ways you can both move forward without hurting one another's feelings. For example, the friend who kept canceling might suggest that they'll make plans with you on weekends, while you agree to understand that you can't get together more than once a month during this busy work period.

PREPARE FOR HOW FRIENDSHIPS CHANGE IN YOUR THIRTIES

When you have more responsibilities in your personal and professional life, your friendships will likely change too. When you were in college, you and your friends might have had different majors and activities, but you were all in a similar place in your life. In the five years after college, that changes and there is a chance you might feel "behind" or even jealous. It can be a lousy feeling because you are happy for your friends but still wish you had what they have. This is a time when some of your friends will move in with their partners, get engaged and married, buy a home, or have kids. If you are still single and swiping on dating apps, in a relationship that isn't moving forward as quickly, or too busy paying off your debt to even think about planning a wedding or buying a home, you might feel like you don't have as much in common anymore.

Try to remember that your friend hasn't changed—she is still the person you went to dinner with every night in college and pulled all-nighters with in the library. (As hard as it can be, try to remember that you are not "behind." There isn't a set timeline for when things should happen, and you'll end up getting there too.) As you and your friends get married and have kids, move, or get big promotions, you will probably see them less often and have less one-on-one time together. That doesn't mean your connection has to be less strong; it just means that the amount of time you spend together and the things you do will probably shift.

Staying In Touch with Friends When You're in a Relationship

Have you ever had a close friend who got into a serious relationship, then stopped texting back or making plans? Perhaps they got so consumed by the relationship that they didn't make time for their friends or even the activities they loved to do independently.

You can have friends, outside interests, and a loving relationship with your partner. They do not have to be mutually exclusive. Your romantic relationship is more likely to be healthier if you both have hobbies, interests, and friendships with other people. Make time for your friends...and don't just text them to make last-minute dinner plans when your partner is on a business trip.

Reach Out More Often

You might not see each other every day or even every week anymore, but try to reach out periodically just to say "Hi" or "I miss you" and see how your friends are doing. Maybe send them a picture that relates to an inside joke, or tell them a funny thing that happened to you. These short messages can show that you care and help hold a friendship together even if you aren't getting together regularly now that you live a few states away or you've been playing phone tag.

When something big happens in your life—perhaps a promotion, move, acceptance to grad school, engagement, or pregnancy—let your close friends know so they can celebrate with you... even from afar.

Make the Trip

Although social media is a great way to stay in touch, it's easy to fall into the habit of *only* checking in online and not connecting in person. Social media is a starting point, but it shouldn't be your only way to stay in touch. Make trips to see each other or squeeze in time to see them when you're traveling for work. Whether you've been texting frequently or just "liking" their posts on social media, you can probably jump back in right where you left off.

Create New Memories

It is really fun to talk about all the silly times you had together in college and laugh about the four of you sharing a tiny dorm room freshman year—but now that you're done with college, it's time to make new memories too. Reminisce about your shared past, but make new traditions like double dates, spending time with their kids, or Friendsgiving celebrations if you are all in town for the holidays.

Points to Remember

📍 If you move to a new city, try new things to meet friends. Join a club and go out with friends of friends.

📍 Friendships naturally change when you leave college. Be ready to adjust with them: Meet up in person when possible and support each other.

📍 If you need to have a difficult conversation with a friend, try to approach it thoughtfully. Tell the other person how you feel, avoid blame, listen carefully, and try to work out a solution.

Chapter 15
Build Your Romantic Relationships

Romantic relationships are a big part of your life, whether you are in a long-term relationship, a brand-new one, in the "so what are we" stage, or are single but going out on dates. This chapter has something for everyone because it touches on some of the main stages of a relationship: dating, making it official, and helpful conversations to have before you get married or commit to a long-term relationship. Relationships are different for everyone—some people have always imagined being married with two kids and a house in the suburbs, some want to be married without kids, and some couples are happy in a committed relationship without saying "I do." Whatever your choose, this chapter has tips for navigating it so you can enjoy a happy, healthy relationship.

HOW TO MEET YOUR "PERSON"

It sounds cheesy, but if you focus on being happy, confident, healthy and self-aware and doing what you love, you'll attract someone who is in a similar mind-set. Instead of looking for someone who makes you feel whole, you are looking for someone who makes your life better, makes you even happier, and encourages you to be the best you can be. So how do you meet that person? Here are some tips!

Dating Apps

Dating apps can be a great way to meet people you might not otherwise meet through your own social circles. You might meet the love of your life or make friends. For the profile, show your personality and talk about some of your hobbies and interests. You're more likely to find people with similar goals and values if you share some meaningful things about yourself.

Do Things You Enjoy

Focus on your hobbies. Join a class or organization so you get to know people over a long amount of time.

Get Introduced by Friends

Just like your friends introduced you to new friends, they could introduce you to the love of your life. The best thing about meeting someone through a friend is that someone has vouched for them and thinks that you are a match.

Be Open-Minded at Group Get-Togethers

If it's too much pressure to go on a blind date, be open-minded about meeting new people at group get-togethers like weddings, birthday parties, and trivia nights. Instead of spending the *entire* night catching up with friends, say hello to the cute stranger on the dance floor and strike up a conversation. These people are all friends-of-friends, so they probably have similar values as the person who invited you.

Talk to People

Okay, this one seems fairly obvious, but people are now on their phones scrolling through *Instagram* or texting so often that actually talking to the person sitting next to you on a plane, waiting in line at the library, or at the coffee shop you both go to all the time is getting rarer. Start the conversation or be open to one that starts. People dated long before dating apps and had really great meet-cutes.

TAKE THE NEXT STEPS TO BECOMING A COUPLE

Whether you met your significant other on a dating app or some other way, when things start to get more serious, it is time to think about where you want the relationship to go. Taking some time to check in with yourself allows you to be sure you're moving forward thoughtfully. Then you'll be ready to talk with your partner.

Decide What You Want

It can be so exciting to meet someone you actually like after what seems like months or years of lousy dates that you don't stop to think about what you want out of this relationship. Before you see if you are on the same page with the other person, think about what you want:

- Ask yourself if this is someone you want to continue dating. Do you have common goals and interests; do you have fun together; are they kind, considerate, and funny?
- Think about what you want. Do you want to have something more casual, where you can see other people without feeling guilty? Or do you want to be exclusive and officially be "in a relationship"?

Know what you want and how you define it before you have the conversation.

TO DO

TAKE STOCK OF YOUR RELATIONSHIP: QUESTIONS TO ASK YOURSELF

Here are some questions to consider as you think about whether you two are meant to be.

- How do I feel when we're together?
- Do I want to be in a relationship *with this person*...or do I just want to be in a relationship?
- What do I like best about this person?
- Do I feel like I can be myself around this person?
- Do I want to see other people?
- How would I feel if they were seeing other people?
- Is the lack of definition stressful or a relief?

Start the Conversation

It's normal to feel nervous about being honest and vulnerable about your feelings, especially in an intimate relationship. Do your best to push past this discomfort—after all, sharing your feelings is likely to lead to much-needed clarity on where you both stand. You might think you are both on the same page, but you might not be...and it's better to find out now instead of hearing that they messaged one of your best friends on Bumble. If you don't want the same thing, you can both move on, and if you do, you'll move forward and be closer.

Instead of using the phrase "We should talk," try starting the conversation on a positive note. You could say something like "I've really enjoyed hanging out these last few weeks, and I don't want to date other people. How do you feel?" You are starting the conversation with a genuine compliment, and you are asking open-ended questions, which invites their response.

Define the Terms

When people talk about being "exclusive," wanting something "casual," or "dating around," those terms can mean different things to different people. Even though it can be an awkward conversation, get it out in the open so you both understand exactly what you mean. Talking about it can help avoid hurt feelings if you find out you had totally different definitions.

Decide If Their Feelings Work for You

You can't control what other people want, but you can control your response to it. It is disappointing when you've started to really like someone and then hear that he or she wants to date around. Be honest with yourself about whether what the other person wants works for you. If it doesn't, walk away and find someone who wants the same thing. If you find that you both want the same thing, then celebrate moving forward.

CONVERSATIONS TO HAVE BEFORE YOU COMMIT TO A LONG-TERM PARTNERSHIP

Strong marriages and long-term partnerships are built on sharing similar goals and values and making decisions together. If you're in a serious relationship, you've probably already started to make some decisions together, and maybe you've even talked about the future. Still, there may be some important topics that you haven't talked about in-depth that will help you find your shared goals and values for the future.

Money

Money is one of the largest sources of stress for many couples, so it's helpful to talk openly about your current financial status and your financial goals. You've already thought of your own financial goals, but now you can set and prioritize your goals together.

To do that, discuss your income and income potential, your savings, your credit score, your debt, and how you will manage your finances. Here are some questions to help spark conversation:

- How much money have we each saved?
- How much debt are we carrying? Will we pay off the debt together or separately?
- Will we have one joint account, a joint account and individual ones, or keep our finances completely separate?
- What are our financial goals for the next five years?
- Would we be comfortable if there is a big gap in our salaries or if one of us chooses not to work if we have kids? Would that change how we make financial decisions?

Children

People usually feel strongly about whether they want children or not, and it's important to agree before you get married, because it's not something people are likely to change their minds about in the future. It's one area where compromise is impossible, so be honest about if you want kids.

These questions can help get the conversation going:

- Do you want to have children?
- How many children would we want?
- Would we adopt or use fertility treatments?
- When would we want to have a baby?
- What method of birth control do we want to use in the meantime?
- How would we make sure we are dividing childcare and housework?

Handling Arguments

Every couple has disagreements and gets into arguments. (If you don't, you're either a miracle couple or avoiding difficult conversations.) Talk about how to stay respectful and kind when you argue, resolve disagreements, have honest conversations about your emotions, and discuss what you need from each other.

One helpful habit is to say "I feel..." instead of "You..." so the conversation doesn't feel accusatory. Avoid saying "always" or "never"; most issues are rarely black and white, and using these terms can feel overwhelmingly negative.

Think about these topics:

- Are both of us being open and honest about our feelings?
- Are there things we can do differently to be kinder to each other when tensions are high?
- Are there things we can do to be more empathetic when we disagree or have trouble seeing the other person's point of view?

Religion or Spirituality

Religion and other spiritual practices may be very important to you as individuals and as a couple. You might have different religious upbringings, beliefs, and customs, some of which you want to keep and some of which you want to change or adapt. Talk about your religious values and beliefs and how you would want to raise your children if you choose to have kids.

These questions can lead you to important decisions:

- What religious or spiritual components will our wedding have?
- Will we go to services together or are we comfortable going alone?
- How do we want to introduce religion or spirituality to our kids?

Sex and Intimacy

When you are in an emotionally intimate relationship, you both feel secure, loved, accepted, supported, and seen. That environment should encourage you to talk about how you give and receive love.

Relationship expert Gary Chapman introduced the concept of love languages in his bestselling book *The 5 Love Languages: The Secret to Love That Lasts.* He identified five ways that people show love and feel most loved and said that understanding each other's love language is a key to a healthy relationship. Check out the book together to see if the ideas can help you connect more.

Ask each other these questions:

- What makes you feel loved?
- What makes you feel appreciated and valued?
- What do you love most about our relationship?
- What turns you on or off?
- What is your biggest sexual fantasy?
- What has been your favorite moment from our sex life?
- What gets you in the mood?

Life Goals

You've made your own five-year plan, and now you get to make one together! Think about where you want to be in ten, twenty, and thirty years. What do you want to have accomplished? What are your career goals? What are your personal goals? Share all your goals for the future so you can work on supporting and encouraging each other.

Check in every few months to see how your big-picture goals are progressing. Take the opportunity to adjust or update goals as needed.

Think about these points:

- What are our personal life goals?
- What do we hope to accomplish in our professional lives?
- How can we best support each other to reach our individual goals—like goals at work—and our shared ones?
- What are our general plans for retirement?

Points to Remember

- You never know where you'll meet your "person." Work on feeling happy and confident and doing what you enjoy—and be open-minded about ways to meet new people.

- Talking about your relationship status can be uncomfortable, but you're both better off sharing your feelings and making sure you know how the other feels.

- If you're in a serious relationship, talking about some big-picture topics—such as finances, children, and life goals—can help you grow closer.

Conclusion

You've come so far since the beginning of the book. You've reflected on your past, thought about what you want now, planned for the future, and created your own five-year plan. This plan will be a road map for the next few years of your life, and it covers all the important aspects: career, finances, wellness, and relationships. It can change as your life changes—check in at least once a month and use the reflection prompts throughout the book to see if any of your goals have shifted.

You've learned the career, finances, wellness, and relationship skills that they didn't teach you in college:

- **Career**: You've identified the right career path for you, mastered the job search, and learned skills that will be valuable through-out your entire career, such as time management, communication, and problem-solving. You've learned how to decrease your stress at work, increase your confidence, build strong working relationships with coworkers, grow your network, and show you are ready for a promotion.

- **Finances**: You've set financial goals, made budgeting a habit, improved your credit score, contributed to your 401(k), and started investing so your money will grow. You've found a place to call home, whether you're living with your parents, renting with roommates, or saving up to buy your first home.

- **Wellness**: You've created a fitness routine, focused on nutrition, found your ideal morning and evening routine, worked on work-life integration, and made self-care a priority. You've learned to treat your mental health as seriously as your physical health and found spirituality practices that work for you.

- **Relationships**: You've strengthened your relationships with family and friends and made new friends. You've focused on your romantic relationships whether you are single, in the early stages of something new, or you've met your "person."

Keep this book nearby and use it as a guide as you navigate your first few years of post-grad life. Be confident and know that you have all of the skills you need to reach your goals and create a life you love.

Resources

CAREER

The Muse: *The Muse* is a detailed job board and site with advice on everything from the job search to landing a promotion. You can find a career coach on the site: www.themuse.com.

Monster: *Monster* is a job board and career advice resource. You can hire an expert to help with your resume and cover letter and use the salary tools to prepare for negotiations: www.monster.com.

Glassdoor: *Glassdoor* is a job board that has company, interview, salary, and benefits reviews, and helpful salary reports: www.glassdoor.com.

Indeed: *Indeed* is a job board with company, interview, salary, and benefits reviews. There are questions and answers with employees and career advice articles: www.indeed.com.

LinkedIn: *LinkedIn* is the best way to share your resume and grow and stay in touch with your network online. It has a job board, salary resources, and interview advice: www.linkedin.com.

FINANCES

Credit.com: Use Credit.com to check your credit score and get personalized advice for ways you can improve your credit score. You can compare credit cards, read personal finance advice, find loans, and more: www.credit.com.

The Balance: *The Balance* has helpful advice on personal finances, saving for retirement, banking and loans, investing, filing your taxes, and more: www.thebalance.com.

Investopedia: Increase your investment knowledge even more with *Investopedia*. It's a valuable resource for learning about investing, personal finance, and staying up to date on the market: www.investopedia.com.

NASDAQ or the New York Stock Exchange: The NASDAQ and the New York Stock Exchange are two of the main stock exchanges. You can use them to check how individual stocks are performing: www.nasdaq.com; www.nyse.com.

Dow Jones Industrial Average or S&P 500: The Dow Jones Industrial Average and S&P 500 are two of the main stock indexes. They are helpful for understanding how the market is doing overall: www.dowjones.com; www.standardandpoors.com.

WELLNESS

Well+Good: Well+Good is a go-to for everything health and wellness. Their website has articles on everything from workouts and nutrition to mental health and relationships: www.wellandgood.com.

SWEAT: *SWEAT* offers different workout programs. The BBG schedule consists of three twenty-eight-minute workouts—legs, arms, and abs—four cardio sessions, one recovery session with guided stretches, and a rest day. There's also a community, ways to track your progress, and healthy recipes: www.sweat.com.

Runkeeper: Runkeeper can help you train for races. You can choose training plans, gets stats during your run, track your workouts, and set new goals: www.runkeeper.com.

Headspace: Headspace teaches people how to meditate. You can search through dozens of guided meditations and track your progress: www.headspace.com.

Verywell: Verywell is a resource for health advice. Check out *Verywell Health*, *Verywell Fit*, *Verywell Family*, and *Verywell Mind*. The articles are written by healthcare professionals and industry experts: www.verywellhealth.com.

RELATIONSHIPS

The 5 Love Languages: This is helpful for understanding how you give and receive love. It's helpful for romantic relationships, but it can also be applied to all the other relationships in your life: www.5lovelanguages.com.

Daring Greatly: Brené Brown is a research professor at the University of Houston and a bestselling author. In *Daring Greatly*, she writes about how vulnerability is integral to difficult emotions like fear, grief, and disappointment, and to the best ones like love, belonging, joy, empathy, innovation, and creativity: www.brenebrown.com.

The Defining Decade: Meg Jay is a clinical psychologist and a narrative nonfiction writer. Her book *The Defining Decade* is about how to make the most of your twenties for work, relationships, and the brain and body: www.megjay.com.

How to Love Yourself (and Sometimes Other People): At the core, this book by Lodro Rinzler and Meggan Watterson is about how you really have to love yourself in order to truly love someone else. It's a guidebook for all relationships, including romantic ones: www.hayhouse.com/how-to-love-yourself-and-sometimes-other-people-paperback.

Acknowledgments

Writing a book takes early mornings, late nights, copious amounts of coffee, and a strong support system. There are so many people who made this book the guide I wish I had when I graduated from college.

Thank you to my agent Leigh Eisenman from MacKenzie Wolf for helping me with the proposal, contract, and advice every step of the way. Thank you to Julia Jacques from Adams Media for thinking of me for this book—it was the most exciting and life-changing email I've ever received. I'm so glad our vision for the book aligned right from the start. I'm so happy I had you to guide me through the process of publishing my first book. Thank you to Laura Daly from Adams Media for the thoughtful edits that made the book exponentially stronger. It takes a team to get a book from proposal to publishing date, so thank you to everyone from Adams Media and Simon & Schuster.

Thank you to my college professors and friends from George Washington University. Writing this book brought back my own college memories. I feel so fortunate to have met so many of my best friends at GW, and especially through Phi Sigma Sigma and Thurston Hall, room 933. It brought me back to my own first few years after college, a time that I was fortunate to meet close friends and mentors, share an apartment with one of my favorite people, and have another one an avenue away.

Thank you to everyone who reads my blog, *Elana Lyn*. I started it shortly after graduating from college because I wanted a space to write about all the personal and professional development topics my friends and I discussed as we navigated our first few years of life after college. I began my career profile series because I felt lost in my career. I didn't know what I wanted to do, so I decided to learn about other people's career paths and gather their advice. It ends up the answer to my own ideal path was there all along—journalism.

Thank you to my professors and friends from Columbia University. I am so appreciative of all of my professors and friends at Columbia Journalism School. The tight deadlines, hours spent reporting, and time in Pulitzer Hall, Avery Hall, and Butler Library gave me the confidence to write a book. I had Paula Span's voice in my head throughout the editing process as I made the writing cleaner and removed the "sludge."

Thank you to my mom, dad, and sister for their unconditional love and support. I'd need at least 100,000 words to say how much you mean to me. An extra thank you to my mom for being the only person who read every single page of the manuscript before I sent it to Simon & Schuster. Thank you for your edits, instilling a love of reading, and showing that it's never too late to create a career you love.

Index